*REVELATIONS FROM HEAVEN IS FILLED WITH WISDOM, INSPIRA-
TION AND FAITH!* I have known Claudia for more than 30 years, and her
words of wisdom and inspirational faith have helped me through many unbelievable crisis situations. She's always had a positive word in the midst
of a storm (when others didn't), and she's always been there for me with a
genuine love, just like the love of Christ. Her teachings and book, *Revelations
from Heaven,* are powerful and positive. The truths and freedom go straight
into my life. Claudia speaks with exceptional clarity, love and excitement—a
love that impacts hearts everywhere she goes!

—COOKIE RODRIGUEZ
AUTHOR OF *PLEASE MAKE ME CRY (OVER 1 MILLION IN PRINT)*

REVELATIONS FROM HEAVEN BRINGS EXTRAORDINARY INSIGHTS.
Claudia Baca-Moore is an excellent teacher with extraordinary insights as
dynamically demonstrated in her book, *Revelations from Heaven.* She capti-
vates her audience with her dramatic style and warm approach. I appreci-
ate Claudia's generous heart and her genuine concern for people. I endorse
her ministry - it has definitely been proven over many years.

—KARI BROWNING
AUTHOR AND HISTORIAN

REVELATIONS
FROM
Heaven

rev·e·la·tion
something revealed or disclosed,
especially a striking disclosure,
as of something not before realized.

CLAUDIA BACA-MOORE
Author of *Awake to Righteousness*

Most ENCOUNTERS PRESS products are available at special quantity discounts for bulk purchase, sales promotions, premiums, fund-raising and educational needs. For details, please email: Publisher@EncountersPress.com or call: (918) 995-2177.

AWAKE UNTO RIGHTEOUSNESS by Claudia Baca-Moore
Published by Encounters Press, Tulsa, Oklahoma
Inspiring Hearts, Transforming Souls; One Book at a Time
Tulsa, Oklahoma, U.S.A.
Printed in the U.S.A.

ALSO BY CLAUDIA BACA-MOORE:
- **Awake Unto Righteousness**
  Learn how God is so much Greater than Your Guilt, Condemnation and Shame.
- **Revelations from Heaven**
  Discover more beautiful facets of our Father God. There is so much more to Him than what traditional religion has portrayed. He unveils His mysteries to those who seek Him out.

Visit the Author's website at: **www.AuthorClaudiaBacaMoore.com**
Cover Design by: ENCOUNTERS PRESS DESIGN TEAM

While the author has made every effort to provide accurate Internet addresses at the time of publication, neither the Publisher nor the Author assumes any responsibility for error or for changes that occur after publication.

As publishers we want to be responsive to the issues that genuinely touch people's lives. One of our primary missions is to publish genuine human experiences, which reflect *authentic encounters with God*; tragedy to triumph, underdog victories and conquests over the impossible. Conjointly, ENCOUNTERS PRESS' teaching and evangelistic books, provides church leaders, ministers and believers with biblical materials that will assist them in their individual missions. ENCOUNTERS PRESS will equip people with the truth of God's Word by *Inspiring Hearts & Transforming Souls; One Book at a Time.*

For a **FREE CATALOG of resources** from ENCOUNTERS PRESS, please contact your Christian supplier or email us at: **Info@EncountersPress.com**.

I dedicate this book to the Father, Son and Holy Spirit:

the Source of all Revelation.

CONTENTS

INTRODUCTION

Why I Wrote Revelations from Heaven

As a pastor and teacher, I have always been aware that the Bible is the written Word of God given to us under inspiration for our instruction in Kingdom living. But I also know that there is more to the Word than just its face value. There are layers of revelation contained in the Bible, and there is also the spontaneous Word spoken by God to us to show us another facet of who He is and who He has made us to be. God speaks this kind of "fresh manna," or "word," to us every day.

In this book I share some of the revelations the Lord has spoken to me, especially that the Words that God speaks to us are Life. There is so much more to God than how traditional religion has portrayed Him. He unveils His mysteries to us as we seek

Him out. In Hebrews 11:6, the Bible says, "Those who come to God must first believe that He is and that He is a rewarder of those who diligently seek Him."

Please join me on this journey to know God more and more. I promise—you will never be the same. As you see Him, you will see yourself in Him. Life here on earth was never meant to just be tolerated until we get to Heaven; but rather it was meant to be lived and celebrated each day. Nothing is impossible for you. God is NOW, and He is drawing you closer to Himself. The finished work of the cross has set you free, and since God has indeed permitted, we will now proceed to advance teachings and understandings of our God. ✲

Claudia Baca-Moore

revelation

epiphany, discovery

1. something revealed or disclosed: especially a striking disclosure
"Then, after a decade of teaching,
came the revelation of His awesome power."

**2. God's disclosure of his own nature and his purpose for mankind,
especially through the words of human intermediaries:**
"Here is an amazing revelation regarding the history of Israel."

3. something not before realized:
"Are you serious? Wow. I didn't know that until this very second!"

PART I

HEAVENLY POSSIBILITIES

"Ah Lord GOD!
Behold, You have made the heavens
and the earth by Your great power
and by Your outstretched arm!
Nothing is too difficult for You."
—2 Corinthians 5:18

HEAVENLY POSSIBILITIES

For a long time, the Body of Christ has been taught and believe that God is a part of us; that we are a reflection of Him. But God is revealing over and over again that we are much more than a reflection. In this time period we're living in, it is vital that we do more than just talk about Jesus—He must be more than merely a part of our life. We must understand that for us to live is Christ. You see, in this day God is not only restoring, He is not only bringing back that which has been stolen, but He is also blessing us with "the spoil." In Old Testament days, when God's people went after the enemy, they not only got back what the enemy stole—they also got the enemy's treasures and possessions. They took everything the enemy had—the "spoil."

You and I are now entering into the time of the spoil. That's how the kingdom of God works. When Jesus uses the term "kingdom of God," He's not talking about Heaven. He's talking about

God's reign here on this earth. And we're finally discovering that we are not just in the Kingdom, but that the Kingdom actually becomes us.

When Jesus went forth, He went with more than a message about the Kingdom of Heaven—He was the Kingdom. Wherever He went, God reigned. He understood that He was the King. He understood that wherever He went, the Holy Spirit would work with Him, bringing about the absolute reign of God in every situation. That's quite a contrast to what we've allowed to happen in modern Christianity. We've become content to live far below what God has ever created us to be. We're content to have a few things work out and say, "Wow, my prayers were answered!" But God has called us to be the pray-er—and that we are the answer.

As we approach a situation (or vice versa), we're not trying to get God to do something. Jesus Christ came to earth with a message and a purpose—to show us the Father. And when Jesus died and resurrected, He came with a new message: "I was the one who was dead. But here I am alive, and I hold the keys of death and the power of the grave." Jesus stripped Satan of those keys. He also said, "There's a power now. The reign will not only be with me, but whosoever I give the keys to will reign." If you were given the key to the city, that means you get to rule the place. Jesus gave us the keys in order that we would rule this place—He wants us to reign on this earth.

Isaiah 45: 8: "Let fall in showers, you heavens, from above

and let the skies rain down righteousness, let the earth open, and let them sprout forth salvation, and let righteousness germinate and spring up as plants do together; I the Lord have created it." He is saying that His absolute purity will rain down from heaven on us that are on the earth, and we will sprout together with the heavenly possibilities! In any situation you're in, there is the potential of a natural outcome, or there are the heavenly possibilities.

NEVER TOO LATE

When Jesus walked the earth, He never expected a natural outcome in a situation. He always looked to the "heavenly possibility." God said, "I've rained it down, now I'm asking you to germinate with it. I'm asking you to come together with it." Same thing today—wherever you go, whatever you experience, there's always the "heavenly possibility." In whatever your situation might be today, what is the heavenly possibility? Understand that nothing is impossible—I mean nothing impossible! When we understand that, we begin to realize that there's always the heavenly possibility. And that it's never too late.

When I think of nothing being impossible, I often think of a very dear friend's story about her youngest child. When she was pregnant, the doctor told her that she had already lost the baby, that it would naturally abort, and that some of the tissue that had already discharged was part of that process. She went back to

work at her job at a nursing home. As she was caring for a woman patient there, she looked out the window and said, "But God,
I don't understand this. You're too late!"

Immediately, a whirlwind came around her straight from
the window. She shouted, "Lady! Lady!" to the patient, trying
to wake her up to see the whirlwind. Then the audible voice of
God said, "I am never too late!" Days after this "whirlwind experience," her pants started fitting her more tightly. She went back
to the doctor, and he said, "Well I don't know what happened,
but the latest ultrasound shows that the baby is in there, whole
and fine." And she delivered her son exactly on his original due
date—right when she was supposed to.

God is never too late. Even when it's past time; even when
the deadline has run out. Even when it's over with—it's not over
with because nothing is impossible with Him. He would say, "In
this Kingdom, this Kingdom in which you and I are kings, there's
always the heavenly possibility."

When Jesus prayed, He told the disciples, "This is how you
pray, 'Our Father, who art in Heaven, hallowed be your name,'"
and in Matthew 6:10, He says, "Your kingdom come, your will
be done, on earth as it is in heaven." In The Message translation,
it reads like this, "Set the world right. Do what's best as above,
so below."

When Jesus was praying, He addressed the Father: "Father,

you're in Heaven, Holy; Holy is your Name. Your kingdom . . ." Then Jesus begins to address something, which concerns us: "Your kingdom come on earth . . ." That's where we are—we're in the world (but not of the world!). "Let your reign come on earth just like it is in heaven, and be manifested in your people." He is praying for the absolute Kingdom of God to be on this earth, exactly like it is in heaven.

HERE IN US

Now the Bible tells us that in the end times, "The glory of the Lord will fill the earth." So we're waiting. "God, we need your glory. God, fill the earth. You promised. You said so in Your Word. I'm standing on Your Word... our glory will fill the earth." Paul puts it this way—he said, "Nothing is to be compared to the glory that is to be revealed on me, and in me, and through me." So where is the manifest presence of God—in Heaven? Yes, certainly—but the manifest presence of God is right here on the inside of us.

How is God's glory going to fill the earth? From Heaven to earth, and then from earth to earth. His glory—in and thorough us. We're "waking up," so to speak, and understanding who we are in Him. We're letting the manifest presence of God infiltrate every part of our being, and so every place that we go, we find "the heavenly possibility".

In Ephesians 1:3, we find Paul's prayer: *"May blessing, praise, eulogy be to the God and Father of our Lord, Jesus Christ, the Messiah, who has blessed us in Christ, with every spiritual blessing given by the Holy Spirit blessing in the heavenly realm."* It's like giving a kid the beautiful train set that he's always wanted for Christmas. It's impossible for him to grab hold of it by himself. He's too little to earn it, purchase it, even to go to the store and pick it up by himself. But it comes to him.

And so that Heavenly realm came to us, and entered into us. He says, "And I have blessed you with every spirit-giving blessing that's in that realm that is now in your realm." In Him, every promise finds His "Yes" and His "Amen." There is not one promise that God is withholding. There's not one promise from God that is waiting for you to "do the right thing" or "jump through enough hoops." There'll *never* be a conversation like this in heaven:

"Hmmm, I don't know, Jesus. What do you think? Shall we give him the blessing?"

"I don't know, Father, they haven't been walking the way they should . . ."

"So what do you think, Holy Spirit?"

"Oh, He's always merciful! Okay, okay, we'll give him a blessing this time . . ."

No! That's not the way it plays out in heaven—He's not withholding anything! I've become the glory of God. And I've become the fulfillment of the promises of God, because I'm born-again, by and in Him. And He tells me that I'm bless-ed—I'm blessed!

Others—they're waiting for Him to bless them. "Father, bless us! Bless us!" Well, as for me—I am blessed. I've been given every spiritual blessing in the Heavenlies, and God said, "Your will be done on earth just like it is here." Every blessing that is in heaven! Healing—that's been taken care of. Any sort of depression—lifted. Whatever is in Heaven, I've been blessed with it here on this earth. And in so doing, God's will is done on earth in this earthen vessel just like it is in Heaven.

THE FIRE WITHIN

In Matthew 3:11, we find John the Baptist baptizing people, saying, "I baptize you here in the river, turning your old life in for a kingdom life." He continues, "But the real action comes next. There's a main character in this drama. Compared to him, I'm a mere stagehand. He will ignite the Kingdom life within you, a fire within you, the Holy Spirit within you, and change you from the inside out."

So when Jesus came, He said, "I've come to baptize you with the Holy Spirit and with fire." Here's what this fire is: He said,

"It's a Kingdom fire; a fire that goes forth to consume everything that is not of the Kingdom." And you are the ones Jesus is speaking about. He's come to ignite a fire in you, to burn out anything that would keep you from the Kingdom.

Jesus was manifest for this purpose, to destroy the works of the evil one. And how does He continue to demonstrate that the works are truly destroyed? Through the fire of the reign of God in every one of us. He said this is what He's come to do. John the Baptist said, "Look, I'm baptizing you with water but this one, this Jesus who comes after me, He's here to ignite you with the absolute reign, the absolute heavenly possibilities, the absolute right and authority that we have in Him."

Now, we've been baptized with the Holy Spirit, but I'm telling you, it didn't stop there. We are baptized with the Holy Spirit, but we've been ignited with whom we are in Him—ignited with the reign. He told the disciples in Matthew 10:7, "preach, saying, "The kingdom of Heaven is at hand."

Now, I want you to imagine this: The disciples go into a town, people are sick, people are hurting, people are demon-possessed and they say, "The Kingdom of God is here."

"Where, where? Oh, shall we get a parade ready? The Kingdom of God, the kingdom is here!"

And the disciples said, "No, the Kingdom of God is here, right here within your grasp. The reign of God is right here for every one of you." And so they went forth with the same message of Jesus: "The reign of God is here. The heavenly possibilities have arrived."

How did the heavenly possibilities arrive when Jesus showed up? **Because** Jesus showed up! He was the one who reigned, and when He showed up, everything changed. The first time He opened up the scriptures, He said, *"The Spirit of the Lord is upon me, because he hath anointed me to preach the gospel to the poor; he hath sent me to heal the brokenhearted, to preach deliverance to the captives and recovery of sight to the blind, to set at liberty them that are bruised, to preach the acceptable year of the Lord."* —Luke 4:18-19.

Everyone said, "Oh, my gosh. We've never heard someone speak with such authority. We've never seen such things!" But nothing was seen. He just simply said, "The Spirit of the Lord is upon me." And He was a man who understood that the Spirit was on Him, and therefore, He reigned.

"Then He closed the book and he gave it again to the minister and sat down. And the eyes of all of them that were in the synagogue were fastened on Him." —Luke 4:20

And He began to show His absolute reign everywhere that He went.

It says in Mark 9:1: "This isn't pie in the sky by and by. Some of you who are standing here are going to see it happen, see the Kingdom arrive in full force." Now, Jesus was talking to His disciples and He said, "I'm telling you"—not only the disciples, but other people—and He said: "There are those who are here who are going to see this come in full force." And for many years the disciples, wherever they went, they would turn the town upside down. What's the last town we've turned upside down?

You know, I'm kind of hoping more people would come to church. I am—so we can get them out of church and into the world. The Bible says, "We're to go into all the world and we're to preach." As it is written in Matthew 28:19: *"Go ye therefore, and teach all nations, baptizing them in the name of the Father, and of the Son, and of the Holy Ghost."*

THE SHADOW OF GOD

And God wanted to show his reign. He would say, "Come under My shadow," and you'd start thinking, "If I'm under the shadow of God, He's right where I'm at, and there could be no foe able to withstand me because He's here." Here is a definition of "shadow" that you are going to like: "to envelop in a haze, in a brilliance, to overshadow." Look at Psalms 36:7, *"How precious is your steadfast love, Oh God. The children of men take refuge and put their trust under the shadow of your wing."* So we say, "Oh Father, I'm under Your shadow, the shadow of Your wing. I know You're right with me and I put my trust in You."

"Be merciful and gracious to me, Oh Lord, be merciful and gra-

cious to me, for my soul takes refuge and finds shelter and confidence in *you. Yes, in the shadow of your wing I will take refuge and be confident* *until calamities and destructive storms are passed,"* —Psalm 57:1. You're in a situation and don't know what to do? Get real snuggly close to the Father and let Him be your shelter. Let Him be the one that you'll stay with until the storm is passed, until things have changed—right under the shadow of His wing.

Psalm 63:7, "For you've been my help and in the shadow of your wing I will rejoice." In Psalm 91:1, *"He who dwells in the* *secret place of the Most High shall remain stable and fit under the shadow of the Almighty, whose power no foe can withstand."* And I like this—Isaiah 49:2, *"He has made my mouth like a sharp sword; in the* *shadow of His hand He has hidden me; And made me a polished arrow;* *in His quiver He has kept me close and concealed me."*

You see every time God's shadow was there—it was for protection. It was for the miraculous. In Luke 1:35, the angel said to Mary: *"The Holy Ghost shall come upon thee, and the power of the* *Highest shall overshadow thee: therefore also that holy thing which shall* *be born of thee shall be called the Son of God."*

This was an impossible situation. A young girl—a virgin, is supposed to have the Christ child and her natural thinking said, "But I've never been with a man." But there was an overshadowing—the very presence of God. There was the manifestation of God Himself, and when the overshadowing came, the impossible happened. No longer was it natural, but it became the heavenly possibility—and she became with child.

God wants you to know something; His shadow is with us, because wherever we are; there He is in the midst of us. In Matthew 17:5, Peter, James and John were taken by Jesus up on a mountain where He was going to pray. Jesus was transfigured before them, His face shone like the sun and His clothes became white as light. Two men appeared, Moses and Elijah, and talked with Him.

And in Luke 9:33-34: *"And it came to pass as they departed from him, Peter said unto Jesus, 'Master, it is good for us to be here: and let us make three tabernacles, one for thee, one for Moses, and one for Elijah,' not knowing what he said. While he thus spake, there came a cloud, and overshadowed them: and they feared as they entered into the cloud. And there came a voice out of the cloud, saying, 'This is My beloved Son: hear Him.'"*

Peter himself, in 2 Peter 1:17, describes that scene—Jesus receiving honor and glory from God the Father, a voice bore to Him by splendid majestic glory in the bright cloud overshadowing Him, saying, *"This is my Beloved Son in whom I am well pleased and in whom I delight."*

Now, I just want you to imagine—you're talking to some people in the cloud. The overshadowing of God comes and says, "This is my daughter, and this is my son, in whom I am well pleased. Listen to Him." You think, "Wow, what an honor, Jesus!" Yes, and John said, "Just as the Father loved me, He loves you."

So, how come I don't have this cloud over me telling you, "Listen to Claudia, she's my beloved daughter in whom I am well pleased"? Where's the cloud? There were outward signs when Jesus walked this earth. But now, when we enter in to Jesus, the same signs that were on Him become living and breathing in us.

Look at Peter in Acts 5:15: *"Insomuch as they brought forth the sick into the streets, laid them on the beds and couches that at least the shadow of Peter passing by might overshadow some of them."* Do you understand that we are so much in oneness with God that his very overshadowing now lives in me? Did you ever see the image of a little boy and when you see his shadow, and it's a huge muscle man? That's us! We are so much one with God that He overshadows through us, that my shadow and His shadow become one. It's the same word. Every time scripture talked about the overshadowing of God where the miraculous came forth, it was because the overshadowing represented His absolute presence, His caring, His love, His mercy, and His kindness.

Peter, simply by receiving Jesus, now contains the Master, now contains the One who is merciful and kind, the same exact word used. They were looking for the overshadowing. The people were looking for the presence of God, and when Peter walked by, there was his shadow. And when his shadow would fall upon somebody, they were instantly healed.

Guess where God's shadow is—it's in every one of us. The shadow of God, the very presence of God emulating through us, it's the out ray of the divine. The Bible says Jesus is the sole expression of the glory of God; He is the light being out ray of the divine. You and I, because of us being in Christ Jesus, now become the expression of the glory of God, the light being, the out ray of the divine.

THE EVERLASTING KINGDOM

When Jesus said, "I was dead, but here I am alive and I have the keys", He didn't keep the keys for Himself. He had the keys to give to us. And He wanted to be the resurrected Christ so we could all be in this Kingdom, and so we could all be the kings just like He said. When the Kingdom arrives, Jesus said, "Wherever you go, say 'The kingdom of God is at hand,'" because when the Kingdom is there, guess what happens—the heavenly possibilities, the miraculous. You never saw Jesus say, "The Kingdom of God is at hand," and everyone went away demon-possessed, full of sickness and hurting and hungry. No. When He said, "The Kingdom of God is at hand," He said, "the reign of God is right here."

Whatever needs to be rained on, He's right here. When the Kingdom arrives, all are delivered. When the kingdom arrives, all are healed. When the kingdom arrives, every situation is turned around. And yet we think that someday God is going to let us have power. "Someday" was 2,000 years ago! We think that someday the situations are going to turn around and change, but the Kingdom is right here—the Kingdom is with you. And wherever you go, you make a decision: be weak and beggarly, be sickly—or be Him. So He told the disciples, "Go forth and be Me."

In Luke 9:11, the crowds got wind of what was going on, and they followed Him. Jesus graciously welcomed them and talked to them about the Kingdom of God. Those who needed healing, He healed. Jesus healed all people. He did not go ask someone else to pray for the sick. He took His place in the Kingdom and simply healed all who needed it.

In Matthew 4:23, He went about all of Galilee, teaching in their synagogues and preaching the good news Gospel of the Kingdom, and healing every weakness and infirmity among the people. The reports spread throughout Syria, and they brought Him all who were sick—those afflicted with various diseases, torments, those under the power of demons, epileptics, paralyzed people—and He healed them. How did He heal them? By the reign of God. The King was in town.

The scepter of righteousness has been pointed to every one of us. And God says, whatever we say, it shall be done. You shall decide and decree a thing and it shall be established for you, and the light of God's favor shall shine upon your ways. When they make you low, you will say there is a lifting up for the humble person. He will even deliver the one for whom you intercede who is not innocent. He'll be delivered through the cleanliness of your hands. It's the truth. Jesus preached, "God reigns," and when He preached, He had that authority. He understood that He was the Word become flesh. He understood the position that He was in, and the rights and the privileges He possessed. And wherever He went, there was healing.

Many came to Jesus' healing hand in Matthew 8:16: *"When evening came, they brought to Him many who were under the power of demons. He drove out the spirits with the Word and restored to health all who were sick."* Understand—everywhere Jesus went, all were healed.

You might say, He went into His hometown and He could only do a few miracles because they didn't believe. That's okay, He went back later and He did all the miracles. When Jesus went back the second time into Nazareth, they were expecting Him. This time they were looking for Him. And I'm telling you, Jesus healed, because there's something about the Kingdom of God.

Yes—there is something about the Kingdom of God, and if you will grab hold of it, all will be healed. Did you know in our ministries there's not supposed to be "Wow, we had this healing and that healing?" All are supposed to be healed. When you go out on the streets, all are to be delivered of demons. Everywhere we go, the situation is not to get better—it's to completely reverse. Everywhere we go, the person is not to leave and go away sick and beggarly and weak—they're to completely change for the better. Jesus never went to a place that it wasn't changed. The question Jesus asked is in Luke 18:8: " . . . *Nevertheless, when the Son of Man cometh, shall He find faith on the earth?"*

Luke 6:19: *"And the whole multitude sought to touch Him, for there went virtue out of Him, and healed them all."* Now, they sought to touch Him because healing power was going out from Him. How often? All the time. And how can that be? Because the King was walking the earth, and the reign of God was everywhere He went.

The Bible says that we once bore the image of the first man, Adam, the earthly Adam. But now we are to bear the image of the second man Adam, the Heavenly Adam. The first man, Adam, was earthly; the second man, Adam, was a healing spirit. So when we first were born into this world, we acted just like the ancestors, just like everybody, we acted just like Adam. We lied, we were deceitful, and we were selfish. But then we were re-created in Christ, and the image that we now bear is a specific image. It's a healing spirit. If you believe you're a healing spirit, then how often can healing go out from you? All the time! People would seek to just touch Him because healing was going out from Him all the time.

So, when the disciples went forth and they said, "The Kingdom of God is here," they were asked, "Where?" But in Luke 17: 20, when asked by the Pharisees when the Kingdom of God would come, Jesus answered them, saying: "The kingdom of God cometh not with observation, neither shall they say, 'Lo, here!' or 'Lo, there!' For behold, the kingdom of God is . . ." (this is ridiculous, we know it's in Heaven) "The kingdom of God is . . ." Right here. "The kingdom of God is within you." It is in your heart and among you, surrounding you. Could Jesus have meant this? It's in me, it's in my heart, and it's surrounding me. The reign of God is not in a geographical place. Here's the place—it's in our hearts. Here is the Kingdom of God.

Acts 14: 22 says that "confirming the souls of the disciples, and exhorting them to continue in the faith, and that we must through much tribulation enter into this kingdom of God." Now, I thought about that for a while. Wow—through many hardships. You might remember reading about John G. Lake. Why did he become so involved in the healing ministry? He started his healing ministry because many in his family were sick and dying. He realized that the same ministry Jesus had, so did he. He realized that healing was given to us as a gift from God, and that healing is a reality of God's Kingdom.

Acts 28:31 says that Paul was "preaching the Kingdom of God, and teaching those things which concern the Lord Jesus Christ, with all confidence, no man forbidding him." He preached about the Kingdom of God to everybody, because he saw that the Kingdom was within us.

Colossians 1:13 says, *"Who hath delivered us from the power of darkness, and hath translated us into the kingdom of his dear Son."* Faith works by love. We're in the kingdom of love—and the Kingdom, the reign of God, is inside every one of us.

When Jesus died, the disciples thought they were going to reign on this earth for their lifetime. They didn't understand—it was a reign for all of eternity, and all of us are in this Kingdom. He tells us in Revelation 11:15 that the loud voices in Heaven said the Kingdom, the sovereignty, the rule of the world has now come into the possession and become the Kingdoms of our Lord and of His Christ, the Messiah. He shall reign forever and ever, for the eternity of eternities. This Kingdom has no end. This Kingdom will always reign, this reigning King will always be the King, and we will always be in this Kingdom where we reign.

In Psalm 145:13 the Psalmist said, *"Your kingdom is an everlasting kingdom. Your dominion endures throughout all generations."* In Daniel 7:18, *"And the saints of the Most High God shall receive a kingdom and shall possess the kingdom forever, even forever and ever."* Now let's look at that again. Who're the saints? We are! So the saints of the Most High God shall receive the Kingdom and possess the Kingdom forever and ever. But just like everything with God: it is offered, it is given, it is paid for and it must be received. I need to receive this Kingdom that's been conferred on me, this Kingdom that's been given to me, and to take my place. We can be like the Israelites that said, "But there are giants . . ." or we could be like the prophets who said, "but they (the giants) are bread for us." We need to understand that we've got to receive this. It's a Kingdom, an everlasting Kingdom.

In Matthew 13:19, "When anyone heareth the word of the kingdom, and understandeth it not, then cometh the wicked one, and catcheth away that which was sown in his heart. This is he who received seed by the wayside." When Jesus was saying, "The sower sows the Word," He says, there's a particular Word that the sower is sowing. It's the Word of the Kingdom, the Word of the reign of God, the Word of the sovereign rule of God. He is saying people will hear it, but if you don't hear it and understand it and make it your own, it'll be stolen from you.

CONFERRING THE KINGDOM ON YOU

Look at Luke 22:29: *"I appoint unto you a kingdom, as my Father hath appointed unto me."* Jesus was anointed and appointed the "King of Kings." He was given the Name that is above every name, and there was a time where God actually said, "This Kingdom is now given over into your hands. I confer it on you." And Jesus received that Kingdom. Now Jesus says, "In the same way that it was conferred on Me, it was just given to Me by My Father, I now confer it on you."

It's as though you're being knighted—He's conferring a

Kingdom on you, conferring a reign that, just like He had, so you and I now have. We become kings. We become those who carry the overshadowing of the Almighty. We become those who, whatever we say, it comes into being. We become those who are reigning in every situation that we come to. We become the Heavenly possibilities. And He says, "I've conferred this on you."

And He told the disciples something interesting. He told them, "I want you to go forth and preach the Kingdom." But let's look at it in Luke 4:43. He said to them, "I must preach the kingdom of God to other cities also: for therefore, I am sent." Now, that is interesting wording. "I must preach the Kingdom of God." It should say, "I must preach about the Kingdom of God." But it says, "I must preach the Kingdom." You know why? He was the Kingdom. He was the reign of God! He was the Heavenly possibility! That's who Jesus was. That's who Jesus is. "To preach" means "to announce, to declare, or to show." Now, how can I show something that I'm talking about, if it's me? Go forth and preach the Kingdom.

Let's see if this follows through in scripture: "And it came to pass afterward, that He went throughout every city and village, preaching and showing the glad tidings of the kingdom of God, and the twelve were with Him," Luke 8:1. Then, in Luke 9:2, "And He sent them to preach the kingdom of God and to heal the sick." How did they preach the Kingdom of God? They didn't have a "felt board" Sunday School presentation. They didn't even have video clips. But they had the Heavenly Possibilities, because that was who they were. And when they healed the sick, they were preaching the reign of God. When they delivered those who were possessed of demons, it was showing forth the Kingdom of God. When they preached with authority and power, they were preaching the Kingdom of God—not about the Kingdom, but showing the Kingdom. He sent them to preach and to heal the sick.

In Luke 9:60, Jesus said to him, *"Let the dead bury the dead: but go thou and preach the kingdom of God."* He says your priority is not to bury your relatives. Your priority is to show forth the reign, the Kingdom of God. It's to manifest God on this earth.

In Acts 28:23, talking about Paul in prison: *"And when they appointed him a day, they came many to him into his lodging; to whom he expounded and testified the kingdom of God ..."* Weird wording— persuading them concerning Jesus both out of the law of Moses, and out of the prophets from morning until evening. But here was Paul in prison, expounding and testifying to the kingdom of God. Do you realize people that were sick came to prison to be healed? People that needed a change in their life came to prison so the Kingdom could be manifest. That's pretty amazing.

Then in Mark 4:11, He said to them, *"To you it has been entrusted the mystery of the kingdom of God."* That is a secret council of God, which is hidden from the ungodly. For those outside of the circle, everything becomes a parable. But to you and me, we've been entrusted with the mystery of the secret of God.

Remember Jesus' message when He came back was, "I was dead, but behold I am alive and I have the keys . . ." Matthew 16:19: "And I will give unto thee the keys of the kingdom of heaven: and whatsoever thou shalt bind on earth shall be bound on earth, and whatsoever thou shalt loose on earth shall be loosed in heaven."

Who has the keys now? The one who is dead and is alive now declares, "I give you the keys." So here we are, praying, "Father, deliver these people. Oh, Father, let America turn to you. Oh, Father, heal all those people in the hospital." And He says, "I've given you the keys of the Kingdom. And whatsoever keys of this kingdom have been conferred on you, whatsoever things you bind are bound; whatsoever you loose are loosed; whoever you forgive, they're forgiven; whoever you set free, they're set free."

Mark 1:15: "...and saying, 'the time is fulfilled, and the kingdom of God is at hand; repent ye, and believe the gospel." Repent, change your mind, and the issues born from regret of past sins; change your conduct for the better. Believe, trust and rely on the good news of the Gospel. That's what we're to say. The Kingdom of God is here. How do you know? Where is it? It's within me. The Kingdom of God is here.

Jesus came back to the earth after dying on the cross, after pouring His blood upon the Mercy Seat of Heaven. He came back for forty days. Wouldn't you be more interested in what Jesus had to say during those forty days than anything anybody else ever had to say? Here's what He talked about:

"To whom also He showed Himself alive after His passion, by infallible proofs, being seen of them forty days, and speaking of the things pertaining to the kingdom of God," Acts 1:3.

When Jesus came back, He showed demonstration and proof by miracles that the King was King forever and always. And when He talked to His followers, He explained the reign of God, the Heavenly possibilities, the overshadowing of God coming forth from all of you, the Kingdom that has now been conferred upon you.   Romans 14:17 says that after all, the Kingdom of God is not a matter of getting the food and drink one likes; instead, it is righteousness—the state which makes a person acceptable to God in heart, peace and joy in the Holy Spirit.

Revelation 1:6 declares, "And hath made us . . ." Who's us? "...Kings and priests unto God and His Father; to Him be glory and dominion forever and ever. Amen."

Revelation 5:10 declares, "And hast made us unto our God kings and priests: and we shall reign . . ." Where? " . . . On the earth." Let your will be done on earth as it is in Heaven. How's He going to reign on this earth? Through the kings. Who are the kings? We are. Accept the call. Accept that which has been conferred. Receive it. He said it's yours.

"For the kingdom of God is not in word, but in power," —1 Corinthians 4:20. God's way is not a matter of mere talk. It's an empowered life. How empowered are you? Are you empowered with everything? Every Spirit-given blessing in the Heavenlies, it's mine.

Then He tells us in Matthew 19:26, Jesus looked at them and said, *"With men this is impossible, but with God, all things are possible."* All things are possible—the Heavenly possibilities, they're right here at hand. Whatever is needed, the Kingdom of God is here. Whatever needs to happen, whatever changes need to be made; the Kingdom of God has been conferred upon us. Every time Jesus went forth, one hundred percent were healed. How many will be healed of the people you're talking to? All of them. Everyone was delivered where Jesus went. Those that needed food, they were provided for because the reign of God was there. It superseded the natural, went into the realm of the absolute impossible, and brought the impossible into the realm of possibility. His will was being done on earth as it is in heaven. How many are going to be healed, delivered and blessed where you go? 🌸

PART II

PLANS& PURPOSES

"Call to Me, and I will answer you, and
show you great and mighty things,
which you do not know."
Jeremiah 33:3

PLANS & PURPOSES

Are you the youngest child in your family? I am. We're often referred to as "accidents." But you can be certain that we were all planned for. Every human being ever born was planned for. God knew you would be here on this particular day, at this particular time, reading this book. And God has great plans for us from here on.

The truth is, our existence has been planned since before the foundation of the world. God—before He ever created the earth, before He ever created Adam—He had you and me in mind. And if He had you and me in mind way back then, He certainly has a plan for you and me today. It's very important that we understand this to be true. Sometimes we'll be in the middle of a situation and we'll say, "God, I just don't know what to do." Well, He knows what to do. It's not like He ever sits up in heaven and says, "Oh, no! I didn't expect that! What are we going to do, Jesus?" And Jesus, with a panicked look on His face, answers,

"Well, I don't know, Father—what are we going to do?" Sounds funny, doesn't it? He is able to tell us exactly what His plan for us is, in every situation. And I love knowing that I've been planned for. I love knowing that answers to problems have already been prepared for me, that God is already on the scene with a solution even before I know that I need one. He makes it easy to enter into His perfect plan for me.

The Bible says, "Do not be conformed to this world, but be transformed by the renewal of your mind. By that we will know what is the good, and acceptable, and perfect will of God," (Romans 12:2). How do I know the plan of God for my life? It's all in the Bible. It's all there, in Him, and He's in us. God has a purpose for everything under Heaven, like His Word says. He has a purpose for all things, and a purpose as to why we're here. I remember when my husband, Wyatt, and I finished Bible College. We wanted to be in the perfect plan of God, and sometimes you get real frustrated trying to find out exactly what that is. "Does He want me to walk this way right now, or does He really have it planned for me to walk that way? Right or left? Fast or slow?" When, in fact, that's not how He directs us at all. He's not trying to control our every move. The Bible says He gives you the desires of your heart. Sometimes we think, "I know if I submit myself to the will of God, He's going to send me to deepest, darkest Africa, and I'm going to be so unhappy." Hey—I'm here to tell you that there are people that have a burning desire in their hearts to go to deepest, darkest Africa. And God will fulfill their desires to do so, just like He'll fulfill your heart's desires!

When we were still a traveling ministry, we were ministering at a church in our hometown of Albuquerque. As one of the pastors began to speak after the music service, he said, "Poor Wyatt and Claudia. We're going to receive an offering for poor Wyatt and Claudia. You might not know this, but they live in a bus. And you might not know this, but they travel into Mexico, minister to all of these poor people in all of these poor places . . . Poor Wyatt and Claudia." As he kept going on and on about poor this and poor that, Wyatt leaned over to me and said, "I thought we were living our dream!" I did, too! I guess our lives and our ministry sounded pretty undesirable to that particular person—but it was our dream. It was in our hearts to do it. And I'm telling you, God will give you the desires of your heart.

When we were trying and striving and seeking God, we asked Him, "What do you have for us? God, what do you have for us?" He'd answer us by asking us, "What do you want to do?"

We'd say, "Not my will, but your will . . ."

He'd ask, "What do you want to do?"

We'd say—humbly, I might add—"Oh, Lord, that's not important. Not my will but your will . . ."

After a few rounds of this, we finally began to understand

that God places desires inside our hearts. Proverbs 16:9 says, "A man's mind plans his ways, but the Lord directs his steps and makes them sure."

ESTABLISH OUR STEPS

In this partnership we have with our Father, our job is to plan our ways and let God establish our steps. In this partnership, instead of begging "Father, plan my ways, we can believe that He already has.

Furthermore, He's put desires—His desires—inside your heart so that your will is in agreement with His will. Proverbs 16:3 says, "Commit thy works unto the Lord, and thy thoughts shall be established." We need to entrust them wholly to him, and our thoughts will become agreeable to His will. Then our plans will succeed. Of course, I'm not talking about plans that are no good, or sinful—evil or hurtful. I'm talking about the things that are deep inside of us.

Since you've been born again, how many of you have, in your imagination, in your wildest dreams, seen yourself doing great things for God? Now, think back to before you were born again. Did you ever imagine doing those great things for Him? Probably not. So it looks like its God—certainly not the devil— that's busy making and inputting these plans into our hearts. It's God.

Every Christian has something inside them that compels them to do something great for God. We were created for the purpose of being in union and in communion with Him. God created us to be worshipers. God created us to be in fellowship with Him. God created us so that He could bless us—and bless us—and bless us!

His loving-kindness is here for us today, no matter what you've done. No matter where you're at, God says, "I see you as perfect. I see you as whole. I see you doing all the right things." He is so loving, so very kind.

"The preparations of the heart in man, and the answer of the tongue, is from the Lord," —Proverbs 16:1. Mortals make elaborate plans, but God has the last word. In other words, He says, "I'm telling you—YOU make these plans."

Wyatt and I wanted to be certain of the will of God, so we'd say, "Okay, Lord, here's our plans…" Every trip we made, we'd say, "God, here's what we plan on doing. We're going to go to such-and-such place, then we're going to go here, and then we're going to go there. If You have something different for us, let us know. But, in the meantime, we'll be busy about Your business." We'd busy ourselves about believing that we'd planned our ways and that He would establish our steps. We'd concentrate on believing that we had entrusted our works to the Lord, and He would cause our thoughts to become agreeable to His will.

When we'd do that, things would happen. Once, we'd planned a foreign ministry trip three months in advance of our departure. We said, "Okay, Lord, we're going to go here, here, and here." So while we were on this particular trip, there were three different occasions when someone we met had a vision of us coming and ministering there six months or more before we got there. Now wait a minute! We'd planned the trip just three months in advance. I know—I remember doing it! So how could these individuals possibly have had a vision from the Lord, seeing us ministering there three months or more before it ever entered into our heads to go there? At one place, a man stood up and called us by our names. Another man in another place stood up and said, "I know what she's going to preach on; I've already seen it. She's going to preach on righteousness." I turned my notes over and I had my interpreter read the title of the message to him—the title was "Righteousness." At the time, I had been researching and preparing that teaching for only a week. Yet God had already broadcast that I would be preaching that message six months before!

Did you know God has gone before you? Jehovah has seen ahead and has already made provision. The I AM has already been there before you ever get there! So when we simply follow Him, our plans and His plans are one and the same. I used to ask, "God, am I planning this or are you planning this?" and He'd always say, "Yes."

Proverbs 19:21 says that we humans keep brainstorming, devising options and plans, but God's purpose prevails. God says, "This is your job—keep brainstorming, keep imagining, keep planning. Then I will establish it. I will turn you to the left, to the right—wherever you need to go—but My plans will go forth and become reality in you." Isn't it nice to know that your plans are God's plans? That God really will put desires inside you? And, that if you're going the wrong way, He is well able to turn you around the other way.

The saying is, "You can't steer a parked car." But you can turn a moving car, even if it's headed the completely wrong direction. So get busy about the Father's business. That's when you'll begin to receive more and more instruction, guidance and counsel; wisdom, knowledge and discernment from Him about how to more effectively achieve your goals.

"Father, I'm just waiting for you to give me the gift of healing and then I'll lay hands on the sick." No—the Bible says, "You lay hands on the sick, and they will recover," (Mark 16:18). Our job is to do what He says. God's job is to bring the results He has promised.

Many times we'll try to wait for something to happen before we step out to do something significant or something great. We're business-as-usual, until the "big break" comes along. "As soon as I win the lottery, man," we say in our minds, "I'm going to start giving money for the work of the Gospel. I'm going to really help my church!" Unfortunately, it just doesn't work that way.

"As soon as God opens the doors of opportunity for me, I'm going to walk through them." And it's true—God does open doors that no man can close. But I'm going to tell you something from my own experience. Many times, the doors that God has opened, we've had to kick down to get through. It's the truth!

We didn't walk into our church building, and then flip a switch, and all-of-a-sudden it was set up like a church. That didn't happen. In fact, we walked into our building with no money, acting like we had money. And we did such a good job of acting that it even fooled the owner of the building, because before he knew better, we were signing papers to buy the building for a price that gave us an instant $78,000 of equity, for nothing down, and no sort of credit check at all!

Okay, it may not have been our acting skills that got the job done. More likely, it was the favor of God that faith in a vision can generate. But whatever it was, the owner of the building believed what we believed. Because as a man thinks in his heart, so is he. And we believed that we had the ability to do enter into that piece of real estate and possess it to do the work of the ministry.

STEPPING OUT IN FAITH

The key is stepping out in faith, not waiting for God to do something more. He's already done everything for us. We're the ones who must appropriate what He has done and take a step of faith—out of our safety zone and into our destiny.

God of the angel armies has planned it. Who could ever cancel such plans? He is the hand that reached out—who could brush it aside? Isaiah 14:27

Whose plans? God's plans. Sometimes we get mixed up, we worry and think, "Well, I missed God on that... You know, last year there was a particular point in time when I should have done such and such." And you know how God is, always ready to chime-in with the "Yes, you should have done such and such, and you didn't—too bad!"

No—that's not how He is, and that's not how He works. Consider Moses. Moses was born and raised to be a deliverer. It's in his heart. Then he sees in his mind an opportunity to begin to deliver his people from the bondage of the oppressor. And, I like what the Bible says about him in Acts—Moses thought everyone would understand the call of God on his life!

Don't make that same presumption in your life. I'm going to tell you—it's possible, maybe even probable, that nobody is going to understand. You know why? Because you don't even understand! It's not guaranteed that anyone else will understand your plan, your vision, your dream—especially when it's still just in your own heart. So don't look for approval of man. The Apostle Paul says, "I do not consult flesh and blood." When I'm taking a step of faith, I don't seek out the opinion of man.

Back to Moses—he steps out and ends up killing a man. And the next day a great judgment from another guy comes on him: "Are you going to kill us also?" So Moses goes and hides for 40 years. "I blew it. You know—if I had just not killed that guy. If I had just not stepped out that way." Now, instead of a plan and a dream, there is great fear and dread in Moses' heart. But God had a plan for Moses' life. Forty years didn't seem to bother God. He still had the same plan for Moses and for His people.

Think about Peter. "I denied Jesus," he must have thought, "All I can do is go back to my old fishing business. I'm not worthy to be a minister." And in that moment, Jesus said, "Okay. I'm going to bless you in your plan." So He told Peter to let down a net, and they pulled in such a great haul of fish that there were too many to handle.

Jesus asked, "Peter, do you love me more than these? Do you love me more than your occupation and its new-found prosperity?"

"You know that I love you, Lord!"

"Do you agape love me?"

"You know I love you in friendship!"

"Then feed my sheep," Jesus said, "Feed my lambs. Feed my sheep."

Peter forgot his purpose. It can happen! He knew that he was a capable fisherman, and he was. His experience told him this. But when Jesus helped him—again—Peter could think about his desire to serve Him. His destiny. And Jesus gave him a choice: the natural or the supernatural.

When Peter forgot his destiny, it didn't cause Jesus to forget his call. When you and I don't move in our call, it doesn't cause confusion in the heavenlies. It doesn't cause Jesus to turn to the Father and say, "We must have gotten it wrong. It must not be within their personality to rise up to the great things we've called them to." No. That doesn't happen.

So Jesus told Peter, "Peter, I've told you that when you turned, you would strengthen the brethren. And now I'm going to show you by which way you're going to be martyred, and I'm going to show you that you will die for me." As we have read in the Bible in several instances, the real desire of Peter's heart was to give his life up for Jesus. He certainly didn't think he was going to be drowned on some fishing excursion, or to die a tired old man. He really had it in his heart to die for Jesus—to die like a man, to give his all in his own estimation. And Jesus gave him the fulfillment of his great desire.

"But those who are noble make noble plans, and stand for what is noble," —Isaiah 32:8. The word "noble" in that verse means "a seeker of God". Those who are diligent seekers of God make it their plan and their purpose. And the prophet Isaiah says we are that noble people.

"Blessed is the man who walketh not in the counsel of the ungodly, nor standeth in the way of sinners, nor sitteth in the seat of the scornful. But his delight is in the law of the Lord, and in His law doth he meditates day and by night. He shall be like a tree planted by the rivers of water, that bringeth forth his fruit in his season; his leaf also shall not wither; and whatsoever he doeth shall prosper." —Psalm 1:1-3.

Everything you and I do—everything we put our hand to—will prosper. There's a reason why that happens: because we don't follow the plans of man. Our desire is for Him. The Bible says He gives us both the will and the desire to serve Him. God will direct your desire towards Him. And when He does, nothing else can satisfy.

In the book of Ecclesiastes, it says that in the heart of man is placed a sense of eternity, which nothing under the sun can satisfy but God himself. When you're approaching somebody that does not know Jesus, you must remember that a desire to know Him has already been placed inside of them. Inside every human being on this earth has a desire that nothing can fulfill except knowing and being with God. They try to fulfill it with this and with that, then with something else altogether. But there's only one thing that can satisfy—God, and He alone.

God has some incredible plans for every one of us. It's not like God has a little plan for you, but a great and grand plan for the person next to you. He has a wonderful, satisfying plan for every one of us. There's something in this life—some major thing—that God has prepared for you to accomplish. And if you don't accomplish it, it won't get done. The work is yours and yours alone.

It is very vital, and it is to our advantage to walk in the paths of God, to walk in His will—to follow His Word. It is very, very much to our advantage to follow Him. It's not just about paying tithes, or about attending church—after all, isn't that what a good Christian is supposed to do? Well, sure—if those things are the result of a life lived for and in fellowship with Him.

Even a born-again, Spirit-filled Christian can try and seek fulfillment in other things. But there's only one thing that will bring true fulfillment, and that is to be in the center of His will. To do what God says to do, and to enjoy the blessings that follow.

"As for me, I am poor and needy, yet the Lord takes thought and plans for me. You are my helper, my deliverer. O my God, do not tarry." —Isaiah 40:17

Notice how many times the writers of the Psalms ask God to think about them. "God, would you think on me? God, would you put your mind on me?" That's because they understand a spiritual principle—whatever person God considers, or is thinking about, it is certain that He has made great plans for them. And God says, "My mind is filled with you." When David writes, "What is man that Your mind is filled with him?" God says, "My heart is filled with you!"

What if we could receive the full impact of the truth that God's mind and His heart is filled with the thought of us? Today—right now! What if you could really believe that God has you tattooed—that's right, tattooed—on the very palm of His hand? What if we really believed that we were the apple of God's eye? What if we really believed that everything He did, He did for you and me? That's how much He loves us.

It just doesn't get any clearer than Jeremiah 29:11: *"For I know the thoughts and the plans that I have for you, says the Lord. Thoughts and plans for welfare, for peace and not for evil, to give you hope in your final outcome."*

God says, "When I think, I plan." And there's a plan that's already been initiated for you before you were ever born. "Accident" or not, before you were ever born, God says, "My thoughts were with you, and I have a plan for your life. I want to see you fulfill every plan."

Here's Jeremiah 29:11 from The Message translation: I know what I'm doing. I have it all planned out. Plans to take care of you and not abandon you, plans to give you the future you hope for.

What a wonderful God! How incredibly wrong it is for us to think that God would make plans to give us something, or make us do something that we wouldn't want. On the contrary—according to His Word, He's the one who fulfills our desires.

SIGNS & WONDERS

When Peter and John met up with the lame man in Acts, they told him, "We don't have any silver and gold, but here's what we do have: in the Name of Jesus Christ, walk!" (Acts 3:6). And the lame man got up, leaping and praising God. Now, you would've thought that after performing a miracle like that, Peter and John would have gotten a great reception. But we know better . . .

But isn't that what we always say—"God, if you'd just do a mighty miracle through me, then everyone would believe in You and receive my ministry." But, just like in Peter and John's day, what we imagine isn't necessarily true. It really isn't!

How many times have people looked at the manifestations of gold dust or the appearance of diamonds or gemstones and thought, "Somebody probably put it there. I'll bet that minister is pulling them out of his pocket." Or they hear the testimony of a miracle healing and think, "That person probably wasn't sick in the first place. It's all in their head . . ."

What I'm saying is this: we think that people will automatically turn there thinking around because they hear about a miracle. But my Bible says that signs and wonders follow the Word. That's why God puts His emphasis on the Word. Signs and wonders inevitably follow.

Back to Peter and John—they had a great miracle happen. A man who had been lame for years is now walking and leaping! But instead of the religious leaders saying, "This is amazing!" they told Peter and John, "But don't ever do that again. We forbid you to preach in the Name of Jesus." This persecution motivates the church to start praying to God "to carry out the plans You long ago set in motion" (Acts 4:28). And while they were praying, the place where they were meeting trembled and shook. They were all filled with the Holy Spirit, and continued to speak God's Word with fearless confidence. Now, that's answered prayer!

And now they're at it again. The church's voice is rising up, saying, "Take care of their threats, Lord. Give Your servants fearless confidence as they preach Your message. Stretch out Your hand to us in power through healings, miracles, wonders—all done in the Name of Your Holy Servant, Jesus."

The church, in the Book of Acts and again today declare, "There is a plan that You've conceived from long ago, and now it's being carried out." God purposed long ago for you and I to be here, now; and for us to carry out His plans. And then, as now, believers said, "As we're stepping in and walking in Your plans that were from long ago, we are seeing that You stretch forth Your hand. And when You stretch forth Your hand, there are miracles. There are signs and wonders. And all we need do is to have the boldness to continue to preach the message."

That's what the will of God is—to utilize the boldness He has given is to speak forth our faith.

JOB'S DISCOURAGEMENT

Job was discouraged. And there were a lot of reasons for Job to be discouraged, don't you think? I mean, not only did a long list of horrible things happen to him, but he also had some really lousy friends! And so Job was down, way down, and wanted to give up. And the folks around him weren't much help. Sound familiar? Sometimes when we're not seeing the fulfillment of the things that we want, we want to let go. But God never does.

When we let go of our hopes and our dreams, the Bible says, 'it makes the heart sick.' But then it goes on to say, "If they are fulfilled—and when they are fulfilled—it's a tree of life." Those trees firmly planted by the water, whose leaves never fail.

Let's look a little closer at Job's discouragement. In Job 17:11, he laments, *"My life is about over. All my plans are smashed; all my hopes are snuffed out. My hope is that night would turn into day; my hope is that dawn was about to break. All I have to look for-*

ward to is a home in the graveyard, making my bed in the darkness."

God comes along and says, "Hey, I want to ask you something, Job. Where were you when I did this and created that and formed such and such? And where were you when I created this 'you,' who are all wise?" And Job's response to God (in Job 42:2) is, "I'm convinced. You can do anything and everything. Nothing and no one can upset Your plans. You asked who's muddying the water? Who is ignorantly confusing the issues? Who is second-guessing Your purposes—I admit it—I was the one! I babbled on about things far beyond me, and made a small thing of Your wonders, which are way over my head. You told me, 'Listen, and let Me do the talking. Let Me ask the questions. Let Me give you give the answers.' I admit it—I once lived according to the rumors I'd heard about You, but now I have it all, first-hand, for my own eyes and ears."

God had to come and convince Job that He was who He said He was. And Job was accusing God of all kinds of things, thinking that there was nothing good that could happen. But then we see the end result of His plans. So remember that you're going to have that same degree of victory in your final outcome and your final times!

I used to look at the story of Job and think, "Okay, You have plans for me, and sometime, one of these days, maybe I'll finally have the victory." But I want to tell you; God has planned and made a way for victory to always be the final outcome in every situation. The final answer is in your favor.

Job 42:12-17 says that God blessed Job's later life even more than his earlier life. Job ended up with 14,000 sheep, 6,000 camels, 1,000 team of oxen and 1,000 donkeys—twice as much as he had when his story began.

He also had seven more daughters and three more sons. He named his first daughter "Dove," the second daughter "Cinnamon," and the third daughter "Dark-eyes." (Aren't you glad he wasn't your dad?) And there was not a woman in that entire country as beautiful as one of Job's daughters. Job treated them as equals with their brothers, and even provided them with the same inheritance. Job lived to see his children and his grandchildren, four generations of them. After 140 more years, he died, an old man full of life.

Job saw victory in a situation that, even by his own estimation, was the worst thing that could have ever happened to him. There was victory, and there was a return. There was restoration, because that's how our God is.

FULFILLING GOD'S PLAN

Job was so totally discouraged that he forgot his plans and gave up his dreams. Job forgot his desire for an incredible life, because all he saw with his eyes was destruction. He gave up on everything. Maybe you've given up on something. Maybe you've given up on a dream. Maybe you think you've gotten too old, maybe you think you're still too young. Maybe you figure that you don't have enough money or you've decided that you've got to manage all of your money better . . .

Maybe, maybe, maybe. But it doesn't matter what your "maybe" is. God never forgets his plans. He doesn't! And His loving kindness, His mercy is here today to tell you that His plan is still in operation for your life.

"Yeah," you say, "I'm fulfilling His plan in some areas, but there are other areas that I'm obviously not fulfilling the plan of God." So how do we fulfill the plan of God for our lives? Receive everything that the Word says. Make it your own. Make everything that the Bible says—make it yours. Receive from God.

Romans 8:28: "And we know that all things work together for good to them that love God, to them who are the called according to his purpose." It says God is our partner everything works together and fits into a plan. Everything we go through, everything we experience, it all works together for good for the plan of God in our lives.

Now I have got to tell you, I don't understand why sometimes there seem to be delays. But God knows.

When Jesus went to raise Lazarus, He told the disciples, "I'm telling you something—for your sake, I'm glad that I didn't come here right away. Now your faith will be strengthened." Let me ask you: what gives God more glory? Lazarus gets sick and Jesus heals him, or Lazarus dies and Jesus raises him from the dead? Which do you think brings more glory to God? And causes more of a commotion?

My friend Manny was probably frustrated that he wasn't getting healed. He told his friends that he had these horrible headaches, and that cancer had come upon him—it was a frustration. I can imagine him saying, "God, why aren't you doing anything? God, I've proclaimed the Word, I've done this, I've done everything I know to do . . ."

And so Manny called me and said, "I think I'm going to die!" And guess what happened to him? He died. But before his next-of-kin had opportunity to pick out a nice cozy coffin for him, he was pulled out of a drawer in the morgue and God gave him life. What's a greater testimony—"I stopped having headaches," or "God pulled me from the drawer after I was dead, and raised me up." Hmmm, let me think . . .

Don't let delays discourage you. Don't let yourself think, "Well I've blown it already"—it's never blown! You will always be fulfilled. God has spoken it, and it must happen. Because God said so. It will all work out to your good—He promises.

"But of him are ye in Christ Jesus, who of God is made unto us wisdom, and righteousness, and sanctification, and redemption." He

says, "This is my plan, that you have not just worldly knowledge, but that you have knowledge from Me." —1 Corinthians 1:30

Have you ever been in a situation where you think, 'I don't know what to do,' and then all of a sudden you get a plan? That's God! His Word says, "Jesus has been made unto you this knowledge." And it says—this is so cool— "Jesus has been made unto us our righteousness." That's what puts us in absolute right standing with God. Because of Him, and our consecration—that which has set us apart for the things of God.

"Well, Claudia, not all of us are going to go in ministry." Hey—all of you are already in ministry!

Sometimes people have a tendency to talk to others as though they have the same desires they do. If I asked you, "What do you think about having a daughter that's a missionary, living thousands of miles away—how does that make you feel?" You might reply. "Oh, I don't know . . ." because, since you don't have a daughter that's a missionary living thousands of miles away, you just can't identify with me. (Just so you know, it's really cool.)

But the identification that every one of us has in common is our life in Jesus Christ. Whether you work a secular job or work full-time in the ministry, it doesn't matter. We are all called "ministers." We are all called "Kings and Priests." We are all called to reconcile people to God, and to show them that

He's holding nothing against them. Every one of us is called a minister. Isn't it remarkable that Jesus is the one who set you apart? And, better yet, we don't have to work real hard at this stuff. Jesus already has!

YOUR FUTURE REVEALED

"Howbeit we speak wisdom among them that are perfect: yet not the wisdom of this world, nor of the princes of this world, that come to naught." —1 Corinthians 2: 6

He said, "There is a high wisdom that tells you the plans of God." Aren't you glad that the Wise One lives inside you? Aren't you glad that there is an unction on the inside of you; that on the inside of you there is the Holy Spirit? One of the jobs of the Holy Spirit—one of His main purposes—is to reveal your future.

I grabbed hold of that truth one time and said, "You're here to reveal my future. Could you reveal it then?" (See, we usually think, "Well, I'll just keep plugging away, and maybe some day something will happen.") But the Holy Spirit says, "I've come to remain with you forever, and to reveal your future." You can sit down with the Father in prayer and just say, "I want to see my future." How many of you have seen your future?

Now here's the advantage of seeing your future: when you're in trouble in the "now," you know that you're going to make it through—because you've seen the future! God wants to reveal the future to you, so you'll know what steps to take towards that future. And, so you'll know that you will make it through anything.

Just between you and me, I'm getting a little concerned. Because in the last vision I had of my future, it looked like I was in my 50's—and I wonder, "What happens after that?" So now I need the Holy Spirit to reveal some more of my future to me. You see, it's been a number of years since He last revealed that future glimpse of myself, seeing that "old lady in her 50's." And the trouble is, fifty doesn't seem old to me at all anymore. What I'm saying is—God wants His divine plan that was previously hidden to us to be revealed to us. There is nothing hidden except to be revealed. There is nothing that God wants to hide from us that has to do with our future.

"For this cause I bow my knees unto the Father of our Lord Jesus Christ," —Ephesians 3:14. Do you realize that God has a plan? And the plan isn't that a few of us come to agree about a few things. God's plan is that the body of Christ will come into a full and complete unity. The Book of John, chapter 17 says, "When you and I are one, as the Father and Jesus are one, then the world will be convinced that Jesus has come."

This is the plan of God.

THE PERFECT PLACE

"And whatsoever we ask, we receive of him, because we keep his commandments, and do those things that are pleasing in his sight."
—1 John 3:22

How do I know I will receive whatever I ask? Because I follow Him, and I follow His plans. He hears us, so we know we have those things that we've asked for. We're in His will.

Not only is this the Father's will, but when Jesus died, He said, "This is My will; I bequeath you My peace." We're in the absolute perfect place that God has for us. The Bible says in 1 John 3:24, "And he that keepeth his commandments dwelleth in him, and he in him. And hereby we know that he abideth in us by the Spirit which he hath given us." They let Christ be a home to them. And they are the home, the abiding place of Christ.

"Hereby know we that we dwell in him, and he in us, because he hath given us of his Spirit." That's what 1 John 4:13 says. I know, that I know, that I know, that God lives on the inside of me. How do I know he lives on the inside of me? I am filled with His Spirit. I speak in tongues. The Holy Ghost is in residence inside of me.

Satan can never convince me that God has "left the building." How funny that he would even try! But did you see in this scripture that Jesus makes His home in me, His permanent dwelling. And then it says something that I think is even more incredible. I make my home in Him—I'm home!

I can now understand what John meant when he said, "I am wrapped in the Spirit." If I'm in Him, then I'm wrapped in Him. I'm talking about being wrapped in God as a glove wraps around a hand—Him in me, and I in Him, making my home in Him.

If you understand that, you'll understand that everything that is Him is in us. Everything that is His is ours, too. Because we're there —we're in Him.

Healing? Not a problem. Deliverance? No hassle. Provision? Abundance? It's ours! Whatever the need—I'm in Him, and He's made His home in me.

I want Him to be real comfortable in me, and I want to be real comfortable in Him all of the time. After all, we've got a pretty nice house, don't you think? Pretty nice!

Psalm 33:11 declares that God's plan for the whole world stands up: *"The counsel of the Lord standeth for ever, the thoughts of his heart to all generations."* All His designs are made to last. God has a plan for this world, and I want to tell you what His plan is. While we say, "God, I need signs, I need wonders, I need this to happen." And God says, "You are my sign. You are my wonder. Now go show forth my signs and my wonders." His plan endures.

THE PLAN FOR JESUS & US

Isaiah 14:26 says that this is the plan planned for the whole earth: "This is the purpose that is purposed upon the whole earth and this is the hand that is stretched out upon all the nations." The God of the angel armies has planned it—who could ever cancel such plans? His hand has reached out; who could brush it aside? This plan is planned for the whole earth.

And it's His hand that did it! God's hand has been stretched out to us; it has not shortened in any way. God has a plan for this world. God has a plan for me. And that plan has everything to do with His plan concerning His Son, Jesus. Isaiah 53:10 said that it's what God had in mind all along, to crush Him with pain. The plan was that He'd give Himself as an offering for sin so that He'd see life and come from it. It's life—life, and more life. And God's plan will deeply prosper through Him.

The plan of the Father for Jesus was for Him to give His life as an offering for my sin. The plan of the Father for us is to receive that offering. In so doing, we're set free from sin.

Some of the saddest things I see in the Body of Christ are Christians who are still trapped in sin, and Christians imprisoned by guilt. The cross says, "Guilt no more. Sin no more." The price has been paid. He's taken care of it all.

Take a look at Isaiah 53:10: "Yet it pleased the Lord to bruise him; he hath put him to grief: when thou shalt make his soul an offering for sin, he shall see his seed, he shall prolong his days, and the pleasure of the Lord shall prosper in his hand."

Was it an ordinary thing that Jesus did? After all, many had died before Him. But nobody had or would live a life pure and holy. No one before or since took on my sin and your sin. It was His will that all the wrath and indignation justifiably meant for us would be poured out on Jesus, so all of God's grace and mercy could be ours.

Jesus wasn't ordinary, was He? No, He wasn't. But I have some news for you. He's in you, and that makes you "extraordinary" as well! That's right, we're not ordinary. There's something different about us. Something outstanding, something special. He lives inside us, and we inside him.

Mark 3:14 says that He settled on twelve, designated them as apostles. The plan was that they would be with Him, and He would send them out to proclaim the word, and give them authority to banish demons. That was the plan for the disciples— they were to go forth to heal the sick, to raise the dead, to cleanse the lepers. Do you think His plan has changed? No, it hasn't— it's just that now He has more than twelve disciples, that's all!

I'm saying there's a very special purpose you're here. There's a reason you're on this earth. And if you think your purpose is to just "hang out and see what happens," you're wrong. Yeah, there's a plan for you. There's a reason you're here. We read in Luke 8:1 that He continued according to the new plan, traveled town after town, village after village, preaching God's kingdom and spreading the message.

THE NEW PLAN

In the Old Testament, when God selected a people and brought them the law, it wasn't so that they should follow it and be holy. The law was given so man could realize he could not ever be holy through his own works, and that he had need of a Savior. So God says, "I initiated the first plan, but now that's been fulfilled by my Son Jesus. Now we're in the real plan!"

Look at Hebrews 8:6: "But now hath he obtained a more excellent ministry, by how much also he is the mediator of a better covenant, which was established upon better promise." But Jesus' priestly work far surpassed what these other priests did, since He is working from a far better plan. In the first plan—the old covenant—if it had worked out, the second wouldn't have been needed. But we know the first was found wanting because God said, "Heads up! The days are coming when I'll set up a new plan for dealing with Israel and Judah. I'll throw out the old plan that I set up with their ancestors when I led them out of the hand of Egypt. They did not keep their part of the bargain so I looked away and let it go. This new plan I'm making with Israel isn't going to be written on paper, isn't going to be chiseled on stone; this time I write the plan in them, carving it in the lining of their heart. I will be their God, and they will be my people."

"But you know, Claudia, I'm so disappointed in things. I'm never going to read my Bible again." Maybe that's what you say—but it's written on your heart!

"I have trouble knowing the Word of God." Really? Read your heart. He says, "I have a plan. And my plan is not something that can be destroyed when commandments written on stone or paper were broken." His plan can't be destroyed because it's written in our hearts!

That's what keeps us doing the things that we do. That's what keeps us in eternal hope—prisoners of hope. No matter how hopeless the situation looks, there's something in us that says, "It'll change!" We understand that there is this eternal hope on the inside of us because Jesus lives on the inside. And we're in the real plan now.

His letter authorizes us to help carry out this new plan of action. II Corinthians 3:6 says that the plan wasn't written out with ink on paper, with pages and pages of legal footnotes, killing your spirit. It's written with the Spirit, on spirit. *"For Christ is the end of the law for righteousness to every one that believeth."* —Romans 10:4

We become righteous. That's what the Bible tells us. It says, "Jesus came and fulfilled every part of that, so that man isn't going to try to be righteous by works, but it's all in Him. That the new plan makes us pure and holy, they make us right." I always think, "What a faith God we have!" It's so wonderful that He can look at us and say that we're "complete" and "perfect"!

"Who, me?" Yes, you! He's talking about you!

What does He see? He sees us clothed with Jesus. He sees us in Him, and Him in us. God always speaks the truth. And the truth is you've been perfected. The truth is you're righteous. The truth is you're holy. The truth is you've been made absolutely perfect and right before God. And if we'd ever receive that, we'd see that which is on the inside—Jesus Christ Himself—fully manifest on the outside!

Hebrews 8:13 says, "...*A new covenant, he hath made the first old. Now that which decayeth and waxeth old is ready to vanish away.*" By coming up with the new plan (a new covenant between God and His people), God put the old plan on the shelf and there it stays, gathering dust. Any time people try to bring in the old; they're bringing in some dusty old thing that no longer has any power or glory with it. Leave it on the shelf!

The old plan was only a hint of the good things in the new plan, says Hebrews 10:1. Since the old plan wasn't complete in itself, it couldn't complete those who followed it. No matter how many sacrifices were offered year after year, they never added up to a complete solution. If the old plan could have perfected you, then we wouldn't have had to have a new one. But the old one died, and so did its benefits. But the new one is Jesus. And He can never die!

And the new dispensation, the New Testament that we're a part of now actually is Jesus. And because Jesus is perfect, then the new thing that we are now in perfects us. The law couldn't perfect us. But Jesus came and perfected us! We had a hint of this redemption through the law, but now we have the reality of fulfillment. And everyone is included in this perfect plan.

THIS PLAN IS FOR EVERYONE

In the past, Christianity has all too often been a religion of exclusion. We apply rules of conduct to say who's "good," who's "bad," who's "in," and who's "out." The people that do "this" are righteous, but the people that do "that" are not! But in God's economy, His salvation is available to all—to all who believe. He wishes all men would be saved and come unto the knowledge of him.

Romans 1:16 says this is news that I'm most proud to proclaim; this extraordinary message of God's powerful plan to rescue everyone who trusts in Him, starting with the Jews, and right on to everyone else. "Well, you know," says the good Christian mother, "my son has rejected it. He's rejected the gospel." But I'm telling you, God says that you and your household shall be saved. And the Bible says that this gospel—this good news, this extraordinary message—is for everyone! He thought of every-thing, provided everything we could possibly need. He let us in on the plans He took such delight in making.

He set it all out before us in Christ, a long-range plan in which everything would be brought together and summed up in Him, everything in the deepest heaven and everything on plan-et earth: Ephesians 1:8. God said everything is involved in this plan—everyone and everything. Read also Ephesians 3:2, "I take it that you're familiar with the part I was given in God's plan for including everybody." Do you know how hard it was for them to preach that the message of God Almighty was not just for a certain nation, a certain group, but was for everybody? Paul was saying, "I hope you understand that my part in this is to give it to everybody." It wasn't exclusive then, and it isn't exclusive now—this isn't a club, it's a family. God wants lots and lots of children. He likes them!   Though Christians like yourself gather in churches, says Ephesians 3:10, this extraordinary plan of God is becoming known and talked about even among the angels. Do you realize the angels are longing to know details concern-ing God's plan of redemption? "How did He come and rescue them? How did they receive? How is He living in them?" Yes, even the angels are talking among themselves about it—even as you're reading this book. They're longing to see and understand the great blessings we've been given.

YOUR SPECIAL ASSIGNMENT

Meanwhile, we've got our hands full continually thanking God for you, our good friends, so loved by God (2 Thessalonians 2:13). God picked you out as His from the very start. Think of it—you're personally included by name in God's original plan of salvation by the bond of faith, and the living truth. God picked you out! By accident? No, I don't think so—God picked you out. He said, "I want you included in my eternal plan." You—one in a million, one in a billion, or more precisely, one in nearly seven billion people alive today—and God said, "Oh yeah, I saw you. I created you! And I want you with me all the time." God has a wonderful plan, loving us the way He does. God has a better plan for us, and you've got a special assignment.

Just like the Apostle Paul, as he said in 2 Timothy 1:1: Paul, an apostle of Jesus Christ by the will of God, according to the promise of life, which is in Christ Jesus. "I, Paul, am on special assignment for Christ, carrying out His plan to lay out the message of the life of Jesus." You've got a message inside you, and you're to present it to the world! You're to take—and to make—opportunities. Whether it seems opportune or inopportune, favorable or unfavorable, you, as a messenger of the gospel, are to preach the Word of God.

In Hebrews 11:40, we see that God had a better plan for us, that their faith and our faith would come together and make one complete whole; their lives in faith not complete apart from us. Now, those "Old Testament guys"—they had some cool things going on. But God had a better plan for us. In 1 Corinthians 6:19, let's examine God's ownership of us: "What? Know ye not that your body is the temple of the Holy Ghost which is in you, which ye have of God, and ye are not your own?" Do you not know that your body is the sanctuary of the Holy Spirit within you? You are not your own, (I love that: "You are not your own . . .") "For Ye are bought with a price," the Apostle goes on to say, purchased with a preciousness, and paid for by His own, made His own. So honor God and bring glory to Him in your bodies.

I'm not mine. So God, put the desire so strong in me to know the fullness, and every detail about what Your plan is. Because I'm not mine, I'm Yours. And I'm glad I'm Yours, because there are some things that need to be taken care of. I'm Yours!

In fact, says 1 Peter 2:9, "Ye are a chosen generation, a royal priesthood, a holy nation, a peculiar people, that you may show forth the praises of Him who hath called you out of darkness into His marvelous light." This tells me more about the plan—He purchased me so I could show forth His wonders by being His sign. *"Remember now thy Creator in the days of thy youth, when the evil days come not, nor the years draw nigh, when thou shalt say, I have no pleasure in them."* —Ecclesiastes 12:1

"Take heed therefore unto yourselves, and to all the flock, over

which the Holy Ghost hath made you overseers, to feed the church of God, which he hath purchased with his own blood." —Acts 20:28.

God says, "I have you set apart for Me, for My will, for My pleasure, for My purpose. You are My reward. I have done this, and I've paid for it with my blood." He bought you. He owns you. And if he owns us, then our owner tells us what to do.

"...I press on and lay hold, and make my own that for which Christ Jesus has laid hold of me and made me His own," —Philippians 3:12b. Do you like this stuff? God likes it! I think I'll be in agreement with Him.

So, Colossians 3:12 tells us to clothe yourselves, as God's own chosen ones, His own picked representatives. Look at how He describes us—as purified and holy, "and well-beloved by God Himself, by putting on mercies, kindness, humbleness of mind, meekness and longsuffering." I'm His chosen one—I'm His picked one. I'm holy and well loved by God. I'm purified.

"Oh, God—just make me pure." He already did.

"Oh, God—I just want to be holy before You." You already are. He did it for you! Whatever we ask God for—it's already ours.

"Ye were bought with a price; be not thee then the servants of men." —I Corinthians 7:23 For He performeth the thing that is appointed for me: and many such things are with him," (Job 23:14). You've just got to know that God performs what He plans

for you. Your job is to connect in with Him, and then you'll surely and without effort perform the will of God in your life.

*"The Lord of Hosts has sworn, saying, 'Surely I have thought,
so it shall come to pass, and as I have purposed, so shall it stand."*
—Isaiah 14:24

*"Having predestinated us unto the adoption of children by Jesus
Christ to himself, according to the good pleasure of his will."* —Ephesians 1:5 It's as though God has a message, as if God is saying,
"I planned for you, I love you, I've given you all that I am, and I
am displaying you so that people can see me through you." The
plan of God—in your school, in your job, in your family, in your
social life, in your church life—make Him to be all encompass-
ing. Make Him your all-in-all. He says, "I'll perform what I have
planned. Together, we will see it come to pass." Of such matters
He is mindful.

Ephesians 2:10 says, "For we are His workmanship, created
in Christ Jesus unto good works which God hath before ordained
that we should walk in them." So that we may do those good
works, God wants the works to be done through His body—
that's us.

You've been purchased, and the price was high. There is a
plan, and the plan is to show forth God everywhere we go.

To look at destruction and see it through God's eyes as absolutely whole.

To look at sickness, ignore the natural ramifications, and see healing instead.

To look at devastation and see the Answer.

There's a good reason we're here. Don't be discouraged in well-doing, for the Bible says, "In due season, you shall reap." Do you know when "due season" is? It's when you need it. That's when we'll reap.

WHEN WE EAT THIS BREAD

Jesus, wanting to show the absolute plan of the Father, said He "desired with desire" to have a last supper with His disciples. And He wanted to have this last supper so that they would never forget what He had done. He told them, "I want you to partake of communion often. If you wait for church to have communion, you'll be in trouble." Every so often we have communion in our churches, but if we only wait for the church to have communion, we're not doing what God said. He said, "I want you to partake, and partake often, of communion."

And He told them, "This is the plan—this bread represents My Body. And here's the plan—My Body will be broken. So when you partake of it, it makes you whole." When we eat this bread, we are saying and proclaiming the Lord's death. And when we proclaim His death we are proclaiming our life.

"I was broken so that you could be made whole. Take and eat of My Body, broken for you." And He went on to say, "This cup cost Me My Blood. But for you—it's called a cup of blessing." And when you partake of it, the Bible says, "His very Blood runs through your veins." The word "cup" means, "lot in life." Jesus said, "I took your cup, your lot in life of wrath and indignation and fears. I drank it for you. And I give you the cup that is rightfully Mine, the cup that I earned. It's a cup of blessing. It's Your New Testament, your new promise."

And He said, "Take it and drink it—it's yours. It's my gift to you."

Let's fully understand this—I'm partaking of this in the natural, but in the spiritual there's something far greater that is happening. In the spiritual, I am proclaiming that He died, and that I am alive. In the spiritual, I am proclaiming that there is nothing—no sin, no charge—against me, because it all went on Him.

The Bible says that before you partake of communion, you're to judge yourself—so judge yourself healed. Judge yourself whole. Judge yourself perfected. Judge yourself complete and perfect in Him. Rightly judge yourself in comparison with the power and quality of His sacrifice.

Because people haven't judged themselves correctly—because they've said, "Oh, I'm poor, pitiful, wretched"—the Word tells us that many are dying early, and that many are sick among you. Let it not be said of us that we partook of communion not understanding and not judging ourselves. Judge the power and authority of sickness as null and void. And judge yourself totally made whole by the blood of Jesus. Whatever it is, judge yourself rightly.

That's why Jesus wanted to have communion. And He wanted us to partake of it often so we could bring it to the forefront of our mind.

Wrath was poured out on Him—I have blessings poured out on me.

He became one with sin—I became one with righteousness.

He became separated from the Father—I am in union with the Father.

He was judged—I'm free. ✳

PART III

THE SPIRIT OF RECONCILIATION

---

*"And all things [are] of God, who hath reconciled us to himself by Jesus Christ, **and hath given to us the ministry of reconciliation..."***
2 Corinthians 5:18

THE LIVING BLOOD OF JESUS

I am going to be talking about the job that we have, to be who God created us to be. God never requires that we do anything that He hasn't equipped us to handle, or equipped us to be. So we are going to begin to look into some aspects of the Word of God on the blood of Jesus.

The message that He's given us is more than just, "This is what I'm going to preach." But, just like Jesus was the Word become flesh, you and I are more than just "I relay a message to you." We become the message.

We are flesh that has become born-again—by the Word of God—born-again by divine seed Who is the Word—and we become the message. We become the Gospel. We become the "good news." I tell you: we are the Spirit of Reconciliation.

As we get ready to do this, sometimes things boggle our minds. But God wants to speak to our spirits, to the hidden heart of man—to the real us. And you have ears that hear, and eyes that see.

You and I were purchased with more than just natural currency, but with the very blood of Jesus. And the Bible tells us—life is where? It's in the blood.

So we were purchased with His very life, with Who He is.

And something interesting about the blood of Jesus: when they would take goats and bulls and lambs and sacrifice them, that blood would be poured out, but soon that blood dried up and they would have to get another animal.

But there's something about the blood of Jesus that is alive, and He never has to be sacrificed again because the sacrifice was good, once for all—the living blood of Jesus.

And so we're going to look at the Word and see what that means for us. Hebrews 12:24, *"And to Jesus, the mediator of a new covenant, and to the blood of sprinkling, that speaketh better things than that of Abel."* It says; "You've come to Jesus, who presents us with a new covenant, a fresh charter from God." He is the Mediator of this covenant. The murder of Jesus, unlike Abel's—whose blood cried out for vengeance—became a proclamation of grace.

The blood of Jesus speaks out a message—the blood is speaking. The blood is saying "there is mercy" and "there is grace" and "there is absolute forgiveness and redemption." The blood is crying out.

BECOMING THE VOICE OF THE BLOOD

And so, if that be true, we should go to where Jesus was crucified, and we should go to the ground there—because that's where His blood was poured out, right? And we should go to the ground there and we should listen real closely.

"Speak! Speak!" No. The blood is still speaking, and the blood is speaking because it has become you and me. The life of Jesus has become the very life that you and I have. And the blood is speaking "mercy," because you and I, as the blood, are saying, 'There's mercy, there's reconciliation, there's peace with God. There is no offense held between you and God!"

And we become the very voice of the blood.

The blood isn't crying out from the ground and telling people a message. The message is in you and me. And we—because we have been born again by the blood of Jesus—we become that voice the blood's speaking. As Christians, many times we have not been speaking the same message. We have not been speaking what the blood is speaking.

"Yeah, they did that? Well, judgment's coming on them!" But let's look at some more Scripture here. Revelation 12:11: "And they have overcome him by the blood of the Lamb, and by the word of their testimony; and they loved not their lives unto the death."

Let me give it to you in The Message: They defeated him through the blood of the Lamb and the bold word of their witness. They weren't in love with themselves—it's not all about them—and they were willing to die for Christ. According to this Scripture, the way we overcome is through the blood of the Lamb and the word of our testimony.

For a long time we thought, "Here's my testimony; I used to do drugs, and I used to do this, and oh—I gave a testimony! Now I'm an overcomer." But the testimony that it's speaking about here is—what is the blood saying? What does the blood testify to? What is the blood saying and proclaiming?

So let me give you some definitions here. "We have overcome" means to subdue, to conquer, to prevail, to get absolute victory. And it says "by the word of our testimony." The word, "word" there means—listen to this, you'll like this—it's "a living voice," it embodies a conception or an idea.

We overcome—we conquer, are victorious—and we become a living voice. The word "living voice" there, is the same as "the Zoe life of God." We become the force—the voice—that speaks life into situations that seem to be dead! Can these bones live? Well, you know. What did He have Ezekiel do? Speak life into them!

And the blood—speaking what? The blood is saying we

become the voice of the blood. "By the word of their testimony" means "concerning future events."

If you have a situation—someone is sick, someone is dying, someone is demon-possessed—the blood is going to speak some future events here—healed. Delivered. Resurrected.

The blood speaks, and is crying out for everything to be brought back into the order that God intended. The Word talks about the whole world moaning and groaning, waiting for the sons of God to be made manifest; waiting for us to take our position, waiting for that blood to speak into their lives. But the only way that blood is going to speak is not through mud, but through these "muds"—through these earthly vessels, through you and me. Hear the following Word with your heart.

"And all things are of God, Who hath reconciled us to Himself by Jesus Christ, and hath given to us the ministry of reconciliation," — 2 Corinthians 5:18,

"That God was in Christ, reconciling the world unto Himself, not imputing their trespasses unto them; and hath committed unto to us the word of reconciliation." —2 Corinthians 5:19

"Now then we are ambassadors for Christ, as though God did beseech you by us: We pray you in Christ's stead, be ye reconciled to God." —2 Corinthians 5:20

"For He hath made Him to be sin for us, Who knew no sin; that

we might be made the righteousness of God in him." —2 Corinthians 5:21.

I love this Scripture, although it has been misunderstood at times to say how God turned His back on Jesus. Nothing could ever be further from the truth. It was God present in Christ who reconciled the world with Himself, not holding their sins against men, but canceling them out, and committing to us the message of reconciliation.

Therefore we are Christ's ambassadors, God making His appeal, as it were, through us. We beg you for His sake to be reconciled to God, because for our sake He made Christ to be sin, Who knew no sin—so that we might become the righteousness of God.

THE MESSAGE IS RECONCILIATION

Now, the blood has a message. And the blood's message is— reconciliation! God is not holding against any man their trespasses!

"But you know the reason God is bringing judgment on America is because of the sin that they're doing." Is that the message of reconciliation?

"Well, let's make some protest signs and go picket some places, okay?" That's not the message of reconciliation.

God's message is this: because I was personally present in

Christ when that blood was shed, I am not accounting against any man—how many men is that? Against any man, that includes everybody—I'm not holding against anybody their trespasses or their sins.

"So I think as a church, we should start pointing out sin . . . Right? Well, if God's not going to do it—somebody's got to do it! Might as well be His body, right?" So He said, "I've given you a ministry—a ministry of condemnation so that you can go and guilt will come . . ." No! That's not what He said!

"I've given you a ministry of reconciliation." We become the Word of Reconciliation. We become the blood speaking, "Be reconciled. I beg you to take hold of the favor that's offered to you."

We begin to see the heart of God that was personally present in Christ, saying, "The way this is going to go forth is through My blood, through the voice of My blood, and through My Word—My people, being My Word.'

Here is 2 Corinthians 5:18-19 in another translation, from The Message Bible: "All this comes from the God who settled the relationship between us and him, and then called us to settle our relationships with each other. God put the world square with himself through the Messiah, giving the world a fresh start by offering forgiveness of sins. God has given us the task of telling everyone what he is doing."

"He's coming back—He's mad at you. We are Christ's representatives!" Once again, no. God uses us to persuade men and women to drop their differences and to enter into God's work of making things right between them.

From The Message, 2 Corinthians 5:20: "We're speaking for Christ Himself now—become friends with God. He already is a friend with you."

How, you ask? In Christ. God put the wrong on Him Who never did anything wrong, so that we could be put right with God. What a message. What a message! That God put us right with Him, and all our wrongs were put on Jesus, and Jesus died.

God has given us the task of telling everyone what He is doing. And we are now speaking for Christ. We become the Spirit of Reconciliation. We understand when Paul says, "For me to live is Christ."

Do we understand that we are living the life of the Spirit? The Bible says that we are living the life of the Spirit. Well, let me tell you what the Spirit's life is—be reconciled! But the Spirit can only speak through these vessels, and therefore being unified and being in oneness with Him we become the very Spirit of Reconciliation.

But because we haven't understood who we were, we've become the voice of judgment. But since we go to a grace church, we're graceful! So we become the voice of reason—But God wants us to be the voice of the blood.

God wants us to be the Spirit of Reconciliation—that's what He's created us to be. Let's look in the Scriptures and we'll see it over and over again—that God has created us to be that.

In Daniel 9:24, it says, *"Seventy weeks are determined unto thy people and upon thy holy city, to finish the transgression, and to make an end of sins, and to make reconciliation for iniquity, and to bring in everlasting righteousness, and to seal up the vision and prophecy, and to anoint the most Holy."*

God told Daniel, "In the future here's what's going to happen. They will set things right. Rebellion will be no more." And see—God has called us to set things right, not by trying to change people's actions but by being the reconciling spirit. By being the voice of the blood.

BEAR THE IMAGE OF THE HEAVENLY

"And so it is written: The first man Adam was made a living soul; the last Adam was made a quickening spirit. Howbeit that was not first which is spiritual, but that which is natural; and afterward that which is spiritual. The first man is of the earth, earthy; the second man is the Lord from heaven. As is the earthy, such are they also that are earthy: and as is the heavenly, such are they also that are heavenly."
—1 Corinthians 15:45-49

And as we have borne the image of the earthy, we shall also bear the image of the heavenly."

Adam became an individual, and the last Adam, Christ, restored the dead to life. The physical life came first, then the spiritual. The first man was from dust; the second was the Lord from Heaven. Those made from the dust are earthly-minded, while those like Christ are heavenly-minded. And as we bear the image of Adam, of dust, let us bear the image of the Man of Heaven.

Now, the Man of Heaven has an image of the Heavenly that it talks about in this particular scripture. It says that His image is a life-giving Spirit. So, if I've been recreated in Christ—if I'm to bear His image—what does that make me? A life-giving Spirit! No longer in the natural—the one of the dust—but from the realm of heaven, and I don't become somebody who talks about the life-giving Spirit, but I have the image and I bear the image.

When He bore our sins, He didn't just take them and kind of reflect them; He became sin. He bore our sin—He bore our sickness!

We bear the image—that means we are not a reflection; it is me—it becomes me. And the image that I bear is a life-giving Spirit, the Spirit that reconciles all things and known to be right with God. Let me tell you what a life-giving Spirit is—in an absolute sense, life as God has it. That which the Father has in Himself, whom He gave to the incarnate Son to have in Himself, the Son has now manifested it to the world—the very life that God has.

Was God ever in weakness at any time? Was God ever in sickness at any time? Was there anything ever impossible for God? You know why? Because He's a life-giving Spirit.

Now, if we'll understand who we've been created to be, we are life-giving Spirits with nothing impossible, with nothing that can overcome us, with no darkness that can overshadow us. But we become as He said, "Just like, exactly like, you bore the image of the earthly, we can bear the image of the heavenly."

We didn't have to work on "how can I be more of a sinner?" It came natural to us. And I'm telling you something: we don't have to work on "how can I be powerful?" Be in the presence of the powerful One, and when we see Him we shall be like Him!

We understand the image that we've been made in.

LIFE IS IN THE BLOOD

Leviticus 17:14 asserts, *"For it is the life of all flesh; the blood of it is for the life thereof: therefore I said unto the children of Israel, Ye shall eat the blood of no manner of flesh: for the life of all flesh is the blood thereof: whosoever eateth it shall be cut off."*

In the laws of Leviticus they did not allow any man to drink the blood of an animal. Do you know why? That's gross, but why else? Because life is in the blood, and if you were to partake of the blood of any animal, the belief was that you were then taking in its life, and would become one with that animal.

And so they could never have any of the blood, because that's where the life was.

The life of every animal is its blood—the blood is its life. That's why God told the Israelites, "Don't eat the blood of any animal because the life of every animal is in the blood. Anyone who eats the blood must be cut off." So, understanding that when they partook of the blood of an animal, they became absolutely one—and whatever the life of that animal was, it would become that person's, and so they were completely cut off.

As Paul said in 1 Corinthians 10:16, *"The cup of blessing which we bless, is it not the communion of the blood of Christ? The bread which we break, is it not the communion of the body of Christ?"* The very life of Christ!

And isn't it the same with the loaf of bread we break and eat? Don't we take into ourselves the body, the very life, of Christ? God sees it this way: "Jesus was taking for Himself the cup of wrath, indignation, and judgment so that we may drink of a new cup. A cup representing our new lot in life, ratified in His blood. You've taken in His life. And the life is in the blood, and every characteristic that is Mine, because that blood was pure and holy—now becomes you. Pure and holy. Limitless."

And so whatever was in the life of Jesus—whatever is in the life of Jesus—that life becomes me. And I become absolutely one with that blood; with the very self-existent life that God has.

"From whom the whole body fitly joined together and compacted by that which every joint supplieth, according to the effectual working in the measure of every part, maketh increase of the body unto the edifying of itself in love." —Ephesians 4:16

He keeps us in step with each other. His very breath and blood flow through us, nourishing us so that we will grow up healthy in God, robust in love. His very breath and blood flow through us. Life is in the blood—and His blood is flowing through us. So whose life is it, anyway?

"And not holding the Head, from which all the body by joints and bands having nourishment ministered, and knit together, increaseth with the increase of God." —Colossians 2:19

They're completely out of touch with the source of life, Christ, who puts us together in one piece, whose very breath and blood flow through us. He is the Head and we are the body. We can grow up healthy in God only as He nourishes us—God's very breath.

When God created man, He breathed, and gave man the breath of life. That very life-giving breath, that very life-giving Spirit now becomes us. And we can breathe life into any situation, because it's His breath that comes forth from us. God breathed into man and he became a living soul. Jesus, after His resurrection, breathed on man, and man became a living spirit.

You and I are living spirits—spirits of reconciliation—that now have the breath of God and we can go forth and breath life into whatever situation that we encounter that seems to be dead.

Jesus came with a very important message. In fact, it was such an important message that He preached it, knowing what the result would be—that everyone would leave Him. But it was the most important message. In fact, when He asked the disciples, "Are you going to go also?" They said, "Where would we go? For You have the words of life!" They weren't talking about different words. They were talking about a specific set of words that manifested the very life of God.

And here they are, John 6:53-56, *"Then Jesus said unto them, Verily, verily, I say unto you, Except ye eat the flesh of the Son of man, and drink his blood, ye have no life in you. Whoso eateth my flesh, and drinketh my blood, hath eternal life; and I will raise him up at the last day. For my flesh is meat indeed, and my blood is drink indeed. He that eateth my flesh, and drinketh my blood, dwelleth in me, and I in him."*

He says that "when we drink His blood" we are appropriating His life. When we partake of Him, then we can bring Him forth. You have heard the saying "You are what you eat"? When we partake of Him we become Him.

Let me give you just the last part of this in John 6:63: *"It is the spirit that quickeneth; the flesh profiteth nothing: the words that I speak unto you, they are spirit, and they are life."* Spirit and life come from us partaking of Who He is, and when we partake of Who He is, we become just as He is; so too are we. And He says, "This is how you have spirit and life.'"

NOTHING BUT THE BLOOD

John 19:34 tells us, *"But one of the soldiers with a spear pierced his side, and forthwith came there out blood and water."*

When Jesus was on the cross, one of the soldiers pierced His side with a spear, and immediately blood and water flowed out. Tradition says that this one soldier, who actually put the sword in Jesus, had some sort of eye problem. And some drops of blood splattered on him, and he was instantly healed. But an interesting thing happened: what was spilled was blood and water—blood for redemption, and water for cleansing. Let's look at it in a different light.

Jesus, Who knew no sin, could not die or be killed in any way because He was sinless. Yet when He became sin (one with our sin), He became mortal, doomed to destruction, doomed to failure—He became death doomed. It was only when He became one with sin that He could actually be physically killed.

And when the soldier went to see if He was dead, out flowed from Jesus that perfect redemptive blood, and out flowed the natural man, born of water that would die; making man no longer just water, but water with absolute redemption, making man unified with His blood. For that which is born of water is of water—is of flesh—and that which is born of spirit . . .

Jesus, the man, died on the cross; Jesus, the Christ—the Spirit—died on that cross. And He said, "Now, it will never be man separated from the redemptive blood. It will never be the holy blood alone, but that holy blood will always be mixed with humanity." Out from Him flowed the cleansing, the water. Out from Him flowed the redemption, the blood—blood for remission, water for regeneration. Blood for atonement, water for purification.

And do you remember why Moses was not allowed to enter in to Canaan Land? Do you remember what he did? He hit the rock twice. (God hates people hitting rocks. You could do a lot of things, but the one thing that offends the Almighty is hitting rocks.)

No. What was it then? Why was striking the tock so offensive to God?

That rock represented Jesus. And Jesus was going to be struck once for all. But Moses added another one to it, and that's why Moses did not enter into the Promised Land, because he added something—something of his own doing, to God's command.

Numbers 20:11-12 affirms, *"And Moses lifted up his hand, and with his rod he smote the rock twice: and the water came out abundantly, and the congregation drank, and their beasts also. And the Lord spake unto Moses and Aaron, Because ye believed me not, to sanctify me in the eyes of the children of Israel, therefore ye shall not bring this congregation into the land which I have given them."*

"And did all drink the same spiritual drink: for they drank of that spiritual Rock that followed them: and that Rock was Christ." —1 Corinthians 10:4.

They all drank from the same spiritual Rock—supernaturally given drink, for they drank from the spiritual Rock that followed them. It was produced by the sole power of God Himself, without natural instrumentality—and the Rock was Christ.

Just like they believed that if somebody drank the blood of animals, they would become like that—we have drunk His blood, become just like Him, with His life. Now the blood, which becomes us—the Spirit of Reconciliation—the voice of the blood that is us—has some things that it wants to speak. And we should always speak in line with the blood, with who we are—because that's how the overcoming is; by the blood and the word of our agreement with that blood; our testimony of that blood.

Hebrews 2:14 reveals, *"Forasmuch then as the children are partakers of flesh and blood, he also himself likewise took part of the same; that through death he might destroy him that had the power of death, that is, the devil."*

Since the children are made of flesh and blood, it's logical that the Savior took on flesh and blood in order to rescue them by His death. By embracing death, taking it into Himself, He destroyed the devil's hold on death.

The blood is speaking out—when it comes to death, Satan's hold has been destroyed. For to be absent from the body, is to be present with the Lord.

"I hold the keys of death, hell and the grave! And behold, I give you the keys of the kingdom."

"Whom God hath set forth to be a propitiation through faith in his blood, to declare his righteousness for the remission of sins that are past, through the forbearance of God." —Romans 3:25

The blood is speaking out that there is Jesus Christ, the mercy seat—and no longer is God holding against any man their trespasses. And God is completely ignoring sin.

"Well, no, He's not! People are in trouble because of their sin!"

Not with God. He hated sin—He did. He hated it so much He became it and killed it.

"And it was for this purpose the Son of God was manifest, to destroy the works of the evil one." And either He did his job, or He didn't.

Either God just put these scriptures here to kid us; you know, "He wasn't joking when He kicked them out of Eden..." But maybe He's joking that He's not holding against any man their trespasses.

Maybe He's acting nice so Judgment Day will be real fun for Him, huh? No.

Jesus is the mercy seat. It is by His blood that we are cleansed and given life. The blood wants to speak something—cleansed, full of life, nothing between you and Me. The blood wants to speak.

Let me give you Romans 3:25 from The Message translation: "God sacrificed Jesus on the altar of the world to clear that world of sin. Having faith in Him sets us in the clear. God decided on this course of action in full view of the public—to set the world in the clear with Himself through the sacrifice of Jesus, finally taking care of the sins He had so patiently endured."

The blood has a message—it wants to voice something. The blood is voicing that God has cleared the world, and has set any charges that the world had, aside. And that they are completely cleared.

Jesus was sacrificed on the altar of the world so that that world would be clear. Where was Jesus sacrificed? Was it this world? Mars? Was it somewhere else . . . no, it was this world.

To set the Christians clear . . . no, to set the world clear!

"Well, they better stop sinning because God's really mad!"

They just don't know that they've been reconciled. They just don't know because the blood hasn't been speaking!

POWER OF THE BLOOD

We thought we'd keep our little secret. But the blood needs to speak.

"That I may know him, and the power of his resurrection, and the fellowship of his sufferings, being made conformable unto his death; If by any means I might attain unto the resurrection of the dead," —Philippians 3:10-11.

The Apostle Paul said, "That I may know Him. . ." and I deeply want to know Him more and more! And that I would know the power that flowed out from His resurrection.

When Jesus died as sin, the Bible tells us He became the "firstborn among many brethren;" or, in other words: the first one to be born again. He had to actually receive the sinless blood—the sacrifice. He was the first one to go from the nature of sin to the nature of righteousness; raised by the Spirit of Holiness—and that same Spirit that raised Christ from the dead dwells in you.

And it is because of the blood that was shed, that was given

for you and me—the very life—, which the Spirit of Reconciliation could come upon every one of us. That we would know that
Spirit of Righteousness, and become one with that Spirit of Holiness, and one with that Spirit of Reconciliation.

The blood wants to say something: "I gave out so that you
could become. I poured out so that you could be poured into."
The blood wants to speak.

"Having therefore, brethren, boldness to enter into the holiest by
the blood of Jesus, By a new and living way, which he hath consecrated
for us, through the veil, that is to say, his flesh; And having an high
priest over the house of God; Let us draw near with a true heart in full
assurance of faith, having our hearts sprinkled from an evil conscience,
and our bodies washed with pure water." —Hebrews 10:19-22

When they would sacrifice the spotless lamb, they would
take the blood and sprinkle it on the Books of the Law and the
people. And when a drop of that pure blood would hit a person,
it was so they could realize they were completely set right—they
had been atoned for, they had been covered up at that time.

But the sprinkling of the blood of Jesus has a different atonement. Sin, not covered up—sin removed. Remember the word
"atonement" means "at one-ment." He became at one with sin
and with failure, with just natural humanity—so that I could be
at one with His Spirit, at one with the life-giving Spirit. At one
with the blood and speaking what the blood has to say.

*"Elect according to the foreknowledge of God the Father, through sanctification of the Spirit, unto obedience and sprinkling of the blood of Jesus Christ: Grace unto you, and peace, be multiplied." —*1 Peter 1:2

Those who were chosen by God and consecrated by the Spirit to be obedient to Christ and to be sprinkled with His blood: May you be filled with grace and peace. The blood wants to speak that there is grace, there is peace, there is deliverance from agitating passions—the blood wants to speak that.

Now, Jesus said, "When you drink of My blood, it becomes everything inside you. And it becomes My life." Not only do I have His blood flowing through me, but according to the scriptures I have it sprinkled on me. I have His blood on me, I have His blood in me, and His blood is speaking through me.   For all intents and purposes, that makes us the blood—sprinkled with the very holiness of God.

*"And, having made peace through the blood of his cross, by him to reconcile all things unto himself; by him, I say, whether they be things in earth, or things in heaven," —*Colossians 1:20.   All of the broken and dislocated pieces of the universe—people and things, animals and atoms—get properly fixed and fit together in vibrant harmonies, all because of His death, His blood that poured down from the cross.

Because of His blood—according to the Father—everything has been made right. But we don't see everything made right . . . But the scriptures say it is! The blood wants to speak so that we can see that which has been done in heaven, is done on earth. So we can see that which God has spoken to be the truth, because we're the ones with the keys.

God's speaking from heaven isn't what's going on right now—God speaking through earthen vessels is what's going on. And when you and I speak what the blood is saying, then we see the victory, then we see everything made right, then we see the life-giving Spirit.

"But now in Christ Jesus ye who sometimes were far off are made nigh by the blood of Christ," —Ephesians 2:13. Now because of Christ—dying that death, shedding that blood—you who were once out of it altogether are in on everything.

How much does God include you? Well, let's see . . . If I've got His blood, if I have His breath, if His love has been shed in my heart and I have His Spirit and I have His mind—I think I'm included in on everything.

"In whom we have redemption through his blood, the forgiveness of sins, according to the riches of his grace," —Ephesians 1:7. Because of the sacrifice of the Messiah, His blood poured out on the altar of the Cross-, we're a free people—free of penalties and punishments chalked up by all our misdeeds. And not just barely free, either. Abundantly free!

The blood is speaking—you do not have a punishment due you any longer; you are set free. The blood is speaking. But it hasn't been speaking through the church the way it needs to, and everyone's afraid of what God's going to think of them. Everyone's afraid that, well, "I better have my fun now before I come to God." Why? Because we've told them—this sure isn't fun! The message hasn't been correct. The Sons of God have not been manifest. And so all of the earth keeps groaning and moaning, waiting for that time.

"And they sung a new song, saying, Thou art worthy to take the book, and to open the seals thereof: for thou wast slain, and hast redeemed us to God by thy blood out of every kindred, and tongue, and people, and nation." —Revelation 5:9

And the new song was, "Worthy! Take the scroll, open its seals. Slain! Paying in blood, You bought men and women, bought them back from all over the earth, bought them back for God. You were paid for. God bought you, and you're to be back with Him." But our message has been, instead—clean it up. And then God won't be as angry.

It's been wrong thinking on our part. This blood that has set us free is not an inferior blood like that of pigs or bulls, but a pure blood from the most holy lamb without spot or blemish. 1 Peter 1:19 says He paid with Christ's sacred blood. He died like an unblemished, sacrificial lamb—and this was no afterthought. Even though it has only lately—at the end of the ages—become public knowledge, God always knew He was going to do this for you. It's because of this sacrificed Messiah, whom God then raised from the dead and glorified, that you trust God, that you know you have a future in God.

"Much more then, being now justified by his blood, we shall be saved from wrath through him," —Romans 5:9. Since we are now justified by Christ's blood, he shall be saved us from the wrath of God. This is the blood speaking—we are now justified. "Well, one of these days..." No—now justified. "Yeah, when I do right things." No!

Let me give it to you another way: Now that we are set right with God by means of this sacrificial death, the consummate blood sacrifice, there is no longer a question of being at odds with God in any way.

You know—God's been a little mad at me. You don't know what I did. I mean, I did something wrong on purpose. And boy—trying to get God to even look at me anymore . . . I'll just kind of wait until He cools down for a while . . .

But the blood is speaking. And the blood is saying, "You're no longer at odds with Me in any way. No longer is it based on action; it's based on blood."   After Jesus died on the cross and resurrected, Mary Magdalene saw Him and said, "Rabboni." But He said, "Don't touch Me, for I am not yet ascended to your Father and My Father." He was going to pour His blood upon the mercy seat in heaven.

Let me ask you a question: Did God accept that blood? If we've become blood, will God accept us? We've been accepted in the beloved. We've been accepted in Him.

Revelation 1:5: "And from Jesus Christ, who is the faithful witness, and the first begotten of the dead, and the prince of the kings of the earth. Unto him that loved us, and washed us from our sins in his own blood." First of all—was Jesus the first one to be resurrected from the dead? No. He was the first one to go from spiritual death to spiritual life, the first one to be truly raised from the dead. Elijah and Elisha saw people raised from the dead, but they died again!

Jesus raised from the dead, never to see death again.

FORGIVENESS OF SINS

And the blood is speaking, and it is saying, "You're loosed and freed from your sins."

"Well, God . . . He wants me to stop doing this and I try so hard, but I just . . . I hope I get forgiveness."

No, He's loosed you from sin. You have more than just forgiveness. You have redemption. You are the Spirit of Redemption.

"Herein is love, not that we loved God, but that he loved us, and sent his Son to be the propitiation for our sins," —I John 4:10: This is the kind of love we're talking about—not that we once upon a

time loved God, but that He loved us and sent His Son as a sacrifice to clear away our sins and the damage they've done to our relationship with God.

Let me ask you a question—does sin do damage to your relationship with God? We just read a scripture that said, "Jesus did away with the damage that your sin did to your relationship with God." But we still have a belief that our disobedience somehow does us in with God. If we'd understand and awake unto righteousness, we wouldn't have disobedience—we wouldn't sin.

"God is not holding against any man their trespasses—except the Christian! Come on—you know that to be true!"

Sure, God forgives all of the murdering thieves in the world. But you missed church last week? You've got to be kidding me! It's on the books, and I'm going to check them twice! You have been naughty and not nice.

God sent His Son to clear away our sins and the damage they've done—past, present and future.

"For the bodies of those beasts, whose blood is brought into the sanctuary by the high priest for sin, are burned without the camp." —Hebrews 13:11

You see, under the old system, the animals were killed and the bodies disposed of outside the camp. The blood is then brought inside to the altar as a sacrifice for sin. It's the same with Jesus. He was crucified outside the city gates—that is where He poured out the sacrificial blood that was brought to God's altar to cleanse His people. The message that the spilling of His blood communicates is—the people are cleansed!

Hebrews 9:12: *"Neither by the blood of goats and calves, but by his own blood he entered in once into the holy place, having obtained eternal redemption for us."* He also bypassed the sacrifices consisting of goat and calf blood, instead using His own blood as the price to set us free once and for . . . a few? Once for the holiest people? No—once for all. If that animal blood and the other rituals of purification were effective in cleaning up certain matters of our religion and behavior, think how much more the blood of Christ cleans up our whole lives, inside and out.

The blood wants to speak: You're clean. Inside and out.

"But if we walk in the light, as he is in the light, we have fellowship one with another, and the blood of Jesus Christ his Son cleanseth us from all sin." —I John 1:7

If we are really living and walking in the Light, as He is, we have fellowship with one another, and His blood cleanses us from all sin.

"Well, when I came to Jesus, every sin that I had done in the past was under the blood. But from then on, the accountant comes out."

This blood is alive. And it's as though it's a Day of Atonement every day, because He is the Atonement. And it's as though it was the day where we got a fresh chance, the slate wiped clean—every single minute of every single day. For His mercies are new every morning.

And the Word says, "The blood of Jesus Christ not only cleansed you from all sin, but it continuously cleanses you, as though it's alive—as though it's a part of you. As though it's there to keep wiping it up and keeping you cleansed from all sin and all its forms and all of its manifestations." That's the blood that becomes us.

Let me give it to you in The Message: "But if we walk in the light, God himself being the light, we also experience a shared life with one another, as the sacrificed blood of Jesus, God's Son, purges all our sin."

The blood wants to speak: your sins are purged. You've been wiped clean. It's taken care of. There's no charge. You're the Spirit of Reconciliation. There's life—the very life of God Himself flows through you. The blood wants to speak.

"For this is my blood of the new testament, which is shed for many for the remission of sins." —Matthew 26:28

"And I said unto him, Sir, thou knowest. And he said to me, These are they which came out of great tribulation, and have washed their robes, and made them white in the blood of the Lamb." —Revelation 7:14.

He said these are the ones who have come out of the great persecution, and have washed their robes, making them white in the blood of the Lamb. You remember when they would take a sacrificial animal and tie a scarlet ribbon around that animal? They would then take part of the ribbon and put it on the door of the temple. When the blood sacrifice was accepted, that ribbon would turn white on the animal and white on the door. That's why our sins—that were once scarlet—are now white. No charge, as though sin had never touched us—as though we were native-born of the light.

WE ARE THE NEW COVENANT

In Hebrews 9:20, The Word clearly states: *"Saying, this is the blood of the testament which God hath enjoined unto you."*

Again in Mark 14:24 we read: *"And he said unto them, This is my blood of the new testament, which is shed for many."*

This is my blood, God's new covenant. Guess who God's new covenant is? It's us! Poured out for many people.

"After the same manner also he took the cup, when he had supped, saying, this cup is the new testament in my blood: this do ye, as oft as ye drink it, in remembrance of me," —1 Corinthians 11:25. As we take communion, we're going to let that blood speak.

The Bible says that we're to judge ourselves—and that

means in comparison with the blood of Jesus. So we're going to judge our situations that don't seem to line up with the Bible. We're going to judge sin as null and void, and the blood's going to speak—sin, you're overcome and defeated! We're going to judge sickness, by means of that blood. He became sickness so that I am full of health. If it's financial—He became poor so that you and I could become rich!

Let the blood speak into your situation—let the blood speak. It's not going to speak from the ground; the blood's not even going to speak from these pages. The bloods going to speak from you. And you've got to let the blood speak—you are the blood!

The only way that the Spirit of Reconciliation will come to this earth is if, by word or deed, we would receive that ministry and become the Spirits of Reconciliation. Jesus desired to have this supper with His disciples, so He could tell them in a nutshell what the whole Gospel was:

"That I became one with sin, so that you could become one with righteousness. That I became one with the result of sin—which was depression, sickness, failure, destruction—so that you could become one with righteousness and holiness—made right.

"Sin not having any hold on you; reconciled to Me, healed, delivered, successful, victorious." Let the blood speak.

"Remembrance" is "to call into the forefront of your mind". But I need you to listen to me—when blood and water poured out from the side of Jesus, it meant that man would never be without redemption, man would never be without the blood—it would always be man with the blood; because forever, He would always be a man.

God says, "In the last days I will pour out My Spirit." The Spirit that He's pouring out is from us—the Spirit of Reconciliation. God's pouring us out like we've become liquid, like the blood.

And He says, "I will pour you out a blessing, that there will not be room enough to contain it." We need to pour out; the blood needs to pour out. The blood, while it was in the body of Jesus, could not redeem man until it was poured out. And it was the blood and the water that was poured out on this earth.

It is you and I—as the blood—that is poured out to this world.

Now I want you to just take a minute and let the blood speak to your situation—right now. Jesus took the bread and He said, "This is My body broken for you." Let the blood speak. What was broken in Him is healed and whole in you. When you've let the blood speak—go ahead and partake.

He said, "This is your new lot in life—this is My blood, and when you partake of My blood, it's My very life." Let the blood speak. You have the very life. Whatever areas seem to be not so lively—let the blood speak.

When you've done it, go ahead and take and drink it. I once heard, "that which goes in must come out." You are the Spirit of Reconciliation. You are the voice of the blood. The blood wants to speak—and it must come from us. ❋

PART IV

KNOWING THE PERSON OF THE HOLY SPIRIT

"The grace of the Lord Jesus Christ,
and the love of God, and
the fellowship of the Holy Spirit,
be with you all."
2 Corinthians 13:14

KNOWING THE PERSON OF THE HOLY SPIRIT

I n the last month of 1990, I had one of the greatest experiences of my entire Christian walk. I had walked with the Lord for about 14 years, and I'd been filled with the Holy Spirit for most of my Christian life. Even back then, I'd ministered for many years and have seen many awesome works of God. I thought I had it all. But as I was praying one day, I heard the voice of the Holy Spirit speak to me. (I want you to know that the Holy Spirit is just as much God as God the Father and God the Son. The three are one, and yet they are three very distinct persons.)

The Holy Spirit said, "Claudia, I'm more than just a power." I replied, "Yes, I know that. I tell people to speak in tongues often." The Holy Spirit said, "I'm also more than tongues. I Am the Person of the Holy Spirit. I have a personality and I have feelings. Yet you treat me as though I am just a power, or as your access to God the Father. I want you to know me. I want to become your closest friend."

As I pondered His words, I was compelled to search the Word of God like never before. And I wrote this so that you may have an encounter with the Holy Spirit as never before—not just a one-time experience, but a full relationship. As you read these words, let them sink into your inner being. My prayer is that my experience and study will help change you from one degree of glory to another, and that the Holy Spirit will become totally real in your life. He will reveal Himself to all who desire Him.

JESUS & HIS RELATIONSHIP WITH US

In 1975, when I first came to know Jesus as my Savior, I had no church to go to. As a three-month-old Christian attending college, I was asked to pastor a work. Besides being a baby spiritually, I was also only 17 years old. I didn't know what to do! I was never taught foundations in the Bible, but I had been baptized in the Holy Spirit. So while I pastored, I determined that I would pray at least four hours a day and hear from God and let Him teach me. I would go into a closet and let God show me things.

The group of students attending the services knew much more about the Bible than I did, and yet God was using me to teach them. It was in my prayer closet that the Holy Spirit began to give me teachings from the Father. I would often bring an unsaved person into my prayer closet and when they would walk in, they would fall down and know that God was there. They didn't even know Jesus, and yet His presence would remain in that place. It wasn't a "magic" room, but God's presence was allowed to be free there.

When you allow the presence of God to be free in your household, people will tell you how they feel "peace" in your home. My prayer closet was the most intimate place I knew of. I brought friends into my closet so we could pray together and touch the heart of God as one. But now I see a new and different flow of the Holy Spirit. He wants to have everywhere we go to be a "prayer closet." When we walk into a room, He wants people to sense the presence of God. This can only happen through relationship with the Holy Spirit—through becoming one with Him. Let the Holy Spirit rule in your life.

In this chapter, we are going to examine the relationship we have with the Holy Spirit. We'll begin with Jesus' relationship with Him: John 3:34 says, *"For he whom God hath sent speaketh the words of God: for God giveth not the Spirit by measure unto him. The bountiful gift of the Spirit was given to Jesus."* Yes, He's the person of the Holy Spirit, but He is also a gift that we must honor. More than as a precious Friend, He is God the Holy Spirit. And we must honor Him as God, with all that we are.

Jesus understood His relationship with the Holy Spirit. Jesus honored Him. The Father God honors Him. *"And the an-*

gel answered and said unto her, The Holy Ghost shall come upon thee,
and the power of the Highest shall overshadow thee: therefore also that
holy thing which shall be born of thee shall be called the Son of God,"
—Luke 1:35 says,

The Holy Spirit overshadowed Mary so she could con-
ceive, and The Holy Spirit brought the Christ into this world.
This was the first time the Holy Spirit and Jesus had an encounter on this earth. Luke 2:26-32 tells us, *"And it was revealed unto*
him by the Holy Ghost, that he should not see death, before he had
seen the Lord's Christ. And he came by the Spirit into the temple: and
when the parents brought in the child Jesus, to do for him after the
custom of the law, Then took he him up in his arms, and blessed God,
and said, Lord, now lettest thou thy servant depart in peace, according
to thy word: For mine eyes have seen thy salvation, Which thou hast
prepared before the face of all people; A light to lighten the Gentiles,
and the glory of thy people Israel."

When Jesus was just a baby, the Holy Spirit was revealing
Him to mankind. The Holy Spirit was opening their eyes and
pointing people to Jesus. And at the age of 30, just before He
began his public ministry, John baptized him the Jordan River.
Luke 3:22 gives the account, *"And the Holy Ghost descended in a*
bodily shape like a dove upon him, and a voice came from heaven, which
said, Thou art my beloved Son; in thee I am well pleased."

When Jesus began His ministry, the Holy Spirit came upon

Him, to have charge of Him. The first charge the Holy Spirit gave Jesus is in Luke 4:1-2: *"And Jesus being full of the Holy Ghost returned from Jordan, and was led by the Spirit into the wilderness, Being forty days tempted of the devil. And in those days he did eat nothing: and when they were ended, he afterward hungered."*

As I first read this, I asked the Holy Spirit why He led Jesus into the wilderness to be tempted of Satan, when the Word says that God will not lead us into temptation (Matthew 6:13). The Holy Spirit said to me, "I led Jesus into the wilderness to defeat the enemy. I gave Him the words to slay the plans of evil and I led Him to victory in the midst of temptation." He'll do the same for us!

I've been in situations that were unbelievable trials. I thought I'd missed God, and sometimes I had. But many times I had not, and I was being led into victory! Many times we see ourselves going from trial to trial, but God sees us going from victory to victory. *"When thou passest through the waters, I will be with thee; and through the rivers, they shall not overflow thee: when thou walkest through the fire, thou shalt not be burned; neither shall the flame kindle upon thee,"* —Isaiah 43:2. If you'll let the Holy Spirit lead you, you'll be oblivious to what Satan sends to destroy you. The Holy Spirit knows the circumstances that are coming, but He also knows His ability to see us through.

When we first rented the building we presently have, I had

seen it during the day and walked through the entire building. Later, I brought my daughter to see it at night, but there wasn't any electricity for lights yet. As we walked through the building, I took her hand and led her. She was scared because she didn't know the way. But she was with me, and I knew the way. We are with the Holy Spirit, and He knows the way! We need to go forward without fear. If we are led into the wilderness, it's only to conquer. Jesus wasn't led into the wilderness to be left alone. He was led there to speak what the Holy Spirit told Him to say: "It is written . . ." It was the Holy Spirit inside Jesus that defeated the devil in the wilderness.

As Jesus went forth to preach, the Holy Spirit gave Him the words and the anointing. He quoted Isaiah 61:1: "The Spirit of the Lord God is upon me; because the Lord hath anointed me to preach good tidings unto the meek; he hath sent me to bind up the brokenhearted, to proclaim liberty to the captives, and the opening of the prison to them that are bound." It was the Holy Spirit speaking that sent Him to bind up and heal, to open eyes and prisons. In Acts 10:38, Paul writes about *"How God anointed Jesus of Nazareth with the Holy Ghost and with power: who went about doing good, and healing all that were oppressed of the devil; for God was with him."* Jesus did good and healed all people because the Holy Spirit was with Him, giving Him the ability. Every miracle accomplished in the ministry of Jesus, was done by the Holy Spirit. Jesus submitted Himself to the Holy Spirit's leading so He could walk in the Holy Spirit's miracle power.

Jesus went through every temptation and trial because He was in fellowship with the Holy Spirit. When Jesus was about to endure the cross, He relied on the Holy Spirit to see Him through. "How much more shall the blood of Christ, who through the eternal Spirit offered himself without spot to God, purge your conscience from dead works to serve the living God?" —Hebrews 9:14. He was able to offer Himself as our sacrifice because of the Holy Spirit, who gave Jesus the ability to go to the cross. The Holy Spirit was with Him!

When Jesus was crucified, the Holy Spirit raised Him from the dead. *"And declared to be the Son of God with power, according to the spirit of holiness, by the resurrection from the dead,"* —Romans 1:4 says. This makes it very clear that the Holy Spirit resurrected Jesus. And the same Spirit that raised Christ also dwells in us.

Jesus was in such a close relationship with the Holy Spirit that He understood the Spirit's workings. Jesus was excited to share this gift with the disciples when He had risen. He came and told them, "I've died for you and been raised for you, and now I can return to the Father so that I can send the Holy Spirit in my place." The Father God and Jesus the Son gave mankind the greatest gift, the most precious gift, by giving us the Holy Spirit to be with us and lead us. Jesus was led of the Spirit—He did not lead the Holy Spirit. We do not lead the Holy Spirit—the Holy Spirit leads us. In prayer, many times I would send the Holy

Spirit to go and do this and do that. The Holy Spirit said to me, "Why are you always telling me what to do?" And I saw that I was trying to lead Him. He's not our servant—we are His. Now, I listen when He says, "Claudia, go and do such and such." Jesus was a successful minister because He listened to the Holy Spirit!

BAPTISM OF THE SPIRIT

"For John truly baptized with water; but ye shall be baptized with the Holy Ghost not many days hence. When they therefore were come together, they asked of him, saying, Lord, wilt thou at this time restore again the kingdom to Israel? And he said unto them, 'It is not for you to know the times or the seasons, which the Father hath put in his own power. But ye shall receive power, after that the Holy Ghost is come upon you: and ye shall be witnesses unto me both in Jerusalem, and in all Judaea, and in Samaria, and unto the uttermost part of the earth,'" —Acts 1:5-8.

Two baptisms are spoken of here—the baptism of water and the baptism of the Holy Spirit. Just as water baptism means to be immersed, so it is with the Holy Spirit baptism. We must be immersed in the Holy Spirit. And when He comes on us, it is not just so we can feel great—it's so we can be effective witnesses. You see, the Holy Spirit knows the heart of God and He knows the hearts of men. He can tell you what to say to reach people for Jesus. *"But the Comforter, which is the Holy Ghost, whom the Father will send in my name, he shall teach you all things, and bring all things to your remembrance, whatsoever I have said unto you,"* —John 14:26.

He's our Teacher. He will teach you and bring to your remembrance Jesus' words when you read your Bible. Here are the very words from Jesus' mouth from John 16:13-14, *"Howbeit when he, the Spirit of truth, is come, he will guide you into all truth: for he shall not speak of himself; but whatsoever he shall hear, that shall he speak: and he will show you things to come. He shall glorify me: for he shall receive of mine, and shall show it unto you."* The Holy Spirit will guide us into all truth by transmitting it from the Father to us. The Holy Spirit doesn't come speaking His own message, and neither did Jesus. We are not here to speak our own message, but the Father's. The only way we can effectively know truth and be witnesses for Him is with the assistance of the Holy Spirit.

The first time we see believers baptized in the Holy Spirit is on the day of Pentecost, after Jesus ascended into Heaven in Acts 2:4, *"And they were all filled with the Holy Ghost, and began to speak with other tongues, as the Spirit gave them utterance."* We see that when they were filled with (or baptized with) the Spirit, the first sign was that they were speaking in tongues. Later, Peter was speaking to some Gentiles, and they were baptized in the Spirit. When that baptism occurred, once again we see that they spoke in tongues: *"While Peter yet spake these words, the Holy Ghost fell on all them which heard the word. And they of the circumcision, which believed, were astonished, as many as came with Peter, because that on the*

Gentiles also was poured out the gift of the Holy Ghost. For they heard them speak with tongues, and magnify God. Then answered Peter, Can any man forbid water, that these should not be baptized, which have received the Holy Ghost as well as we?" —Acts 10:44-47.

SPEAKING IN TONGUES

Later in the Book of Acts, we read that the Apostle Paul encountered a group of Christians who were not baptized in the Holy Spirit. In fact, they hadn't even heard of the Holy Spirit. But once they received the baptism in the Holy Spirit, they too spoke in other tongues. Picking up the story in Acts 19:2-6: *"He said unto them, Have ye received the Holy Ghost since ye believed? And they said unto him, We have not so much as heard whether there be any Holy Ghost. And he said unto them, Unto what then were ye baptized? And they said, Unto John's baptism. Then said Paul, John verily baptized with the baptism of repentance, saying unto the people, that they should believe on him, which should come after him, that is, on Christ Jesus. When they heard this, they were baptized in the name of the Lord Jesus. And when Paul had laid his hands upon them, the Holy Ghost came on them; and they spake with tongues, and prophesied."*

Many people wonder about tongues. They ask, "Who can receive them, and why?" As we see, believers in Acts Chapter 2 received the Holy Spirit. What happened? They spoke in other tongues! "Tongues" is simply a language, unknown to the speaker, which speaks directly to God. Sometimes we don't know how to pray in a situation, but the Holy Spirit can pray through us. Let's look at 1 Corinthians 14:2, *"For he that speaketh in an unknown tongue speaketh not unto men, but unto God: for no man understandeth him; howbeit in the spirit he speaketh mysteries."*

We are speaking directly to the Father in perfect line with His will. The speaker doesn't know what is being said, but the Holy Spirit and the Father does. When you pray in tongues, you pray perfect prayers and you feel His power as you pray. 1 Corinthians 14:4 says, *"He that speaketh in an unknown tongue edifieth himself; but he that prophesieth edifieth the church."* We are built up in the Spirit when we pray in tongues.

Several key benefits occur when the believer speaks in tongues. We see in 1 Corinthians 14:2 that, *"For he that speaketh in an unknown tongue speaketh not unto men, but unto God: for no man understandeth him; howbeit in the spirit he speaketh mysteries."* We utter secret truths, and God hears our perfect prayers. Sometimes I don't know how or what to pray in a certain situation, but I know I can just begin to pray in tongues—and I feel great! In Jude verse 20, we see another reason that praying in the Spirit is to our advantage: *"But ye, beloved, building up yourselves on your most holy faith, praying in the Holy Ghost. Keep yourselves in the love of God, looking for the mercy of our Lord Jesus Christ unto eternal life."* —Jude 1:20-21. We build up our faith when we pray in tongues, and when we do; the Holy Spirit gives each believer a prayer language through which we speak directly to God.

The question is often asked, "Do I have to speak in tongues in order to have the Holy Spirit?" That question bothers me. It's like saying, "Do I have to spend my millions of dollars to have lots of nice things?" Well, to have all the things you desire and to have the full value of your money, yes, you do have to spend it. You can just let it sit dormant if you wish, but what a terrible waste! The same is true with the Holy Spirit. He won't make you speak in tongues, but when He comes in you, He gives you the ability to speak. So, yes, you can have the Holy Spirit and not speak in tongues. But what a waste of potential power and ability.

Let's look at who has a right to speak in tongues. 1 Corinthians 12:7 says, *"But the manifestation of the Spirit is given to every man to profit withal."* The word "manifestation" means "initial sign." If I were to cut my hand, the initial sign would be pain. That would be the first thing that would happen.

So let's look in the Word to see what was the first thing that happened in Acts, Chapter 2, when they received the Holy Spirit. It says they spoke in tongues, which is what happens each and every time someone receives the Holy Spirit in the Bible:

"And it came to pass, that, while Apollos was at Corinth, Paul having passed through the upper coasts came to Ephesus: and finding certain disciples, He said unto them, 'Have ye received the Holy Ghost

since ye believed?' And they said unto him, 'We have not so much as heard whether there be any Holy Ghost.' And he said unto them, 'Unto what then were ye baptized?' And they said, 'Unto John's baptism.' Then said Paul, 'John verily baptized with the baptism of repentance, saying unto the people, that they should believe on him which should come after him, that is, on Christ Jesus.' When they heard this, they were baptized in the name of the Lord Jesus. And when Paul had laid his hands upon them, the Holy Ghost came on them; and they spake with tongues, and prophesied." —Acts 19:1-6.

These were believers who received the Holy Spirit, and the initial sign was that they spoke in tongues. Mark 16:17 says, *"And these signs shall follow them that believe; In my name shall they cast out devils; they shall speak with new tongues."* If you're a believer in the name of Jesus, you can drive out demons and speak in new languages. It's your right as a believer. Some say, "Well, tongues is the least of the gifts"—but, hey, you've got to start somewhere!

Let me clear up some confusion here. The Bible says clearly that not all will have the gift of tongues (1 Corinthians 12:30). Yet, here I am teaching that all can speak in tongues! You see there is a difference between the "gift of tongues" and "speaking in tongues".

The "gift of tongues" is used when the body of Christ gets together. In the church, someone may get up and speak a message in tongues for an interpretation to follow. That's most useful during public worship.

But the prayer tongue (or language), also referred to as "speaking in tongues", is for every believer. Our individual prayer language is not for the edification of the church as a group; it is for ourselves.

If you've not received the Holy Spirit with the evidence and manifestation of tongues, you can right now. If you're a believer in Jesus, you know that Jesus came to this world, died, and rose again from the dead for you. You believe in Jesus in your heart and have confessed Him with your mouth—you are saved. And, as a believer, you can ask for the Holy Spirit and He will come and baptize you, and you will speak in tongues.

"Well, how will I know what to say?" The Holy Spirit will give you utterance. Normally, your words come from your head to your mouth. But with your new language, it comes from your belly (spirit) to your head, and then to your mouth. *"For out of your belly shall flow rivers of living waters,"* —John 7:38. The Spirit lives in our innermost being. He will not force you to speak in tongues, but rather he will empower you to do so. Ask the Holy Spirit to come into you. Breathe Him in, and begin to speak the words He gives you. We simply ask God to baptize us with His Spirit, and enable us to speak in tongues, and He does it. Speak in tongues often!

GIFTS OF THE HOLY SPIRIT

"Now concerning spiritual gifts, brethren, I would not have you ignorant. Ye know that ye were Gentiles, carried away unto these dumb idols, even as ye were led. Wherefore I give you to understand, that no man speaking by the Spirit of God calleth Jesus accursed: and that no man can say that Jesus is the Lord, but by the Holy Ghost.

"Now there are diversities of gifts, but the same Spirit. And there are differences of administrations, but the same Lord. And there are diversities of operations, but it is the same God, which worketh all in all. But the manifestation of the Spirit is given to every man to profit withal.

"For to one is given by the Spirit the word of wisdom; to another the word of knowledge by the same Spirit; To another faith by the same Spirit; to another the gifts of healing by the same Spirit; To another the working of miracles; to another prophecy; to another discerning of spirits; to another divers kinds of tongues; to another the interpretation of tongues," —1 Corinthians 12:1-10.

We must study so we are not misinformed about the gifts of the Spirit. As we read these passages of scripture, we feel somewhat helpless because it tells us that the operation of these gifts is as the Spirit wills. We infer, by reference to our own personal experiences, that the Spirit willed for some to operate in a gift, but not others. But this notion is inconsistent with the personality of the Holy Spirit. The Holy Spirit's will is the same, as the Father

God's will—the One who wills all to be healed. We understand the Scripture that says, "For it is God's will that all be saved."

Let's put it in another way. God wishes that all be saved as He wills. Someone says, "Well, salvation is as God wills—some to be saved and some not to be." But we know that its God's will that all be saved. In the same way, it is the Holy Spirit's will that we all move in His gifts. Verse 11 in 1 Corinthians 12 says, *"But all these worketh that one and the selfsame Spirit, dividing to every man severally as he will."* Jesus moved in all the gifts. Paul moved in all the gifts. We can move in all the gifts.

A person will say, "I have the gift of healing." I understand what they're referring to, but that's not right—because the gift of healing is for someone who is sick. We are vessels for the gifts to move through. We don't "possess" the gift—we give it out! Choose the gifts you would like to operate in, and pursue it according to 1 Corinthians 12:31: *"But covet earnestly the best gifts: and yet show I unto you a more excellent way."*

Let me give you the definition and an example of each spiritual gift that's listed in 1 Corinthians 12:

Word of Wisdom

An insight into the divine will of God, showing how to solve a problem:

"And Elijah the Tishbite, who was of the inhabitants of Gilead,

said unto Ahab, As the Lord God of Israel liveth, before whom I stand, there shall not be dew nor rain these years, but according to my word.

"And the word of the Lord came unto him, saying, Get thee hence, and turn thee eastward, and hide thyself by the brook Cherith, which is before Jordan. And it shall be, that thou shalt drink of the brook; and I have commanded the ravens to feed thee there.

"So he went and did according unto the word of the Lord: for he went and dwelt by the brook Cherith that is before Jordan. And the ravens brought him bread and flesh in the morning, and bread and flesh in the evening; and he drank of the brook," —1 Kings 17:1-6.

Word of Knowledge

A revelation or insight into God's knowledge:

"The woman answered and said, I have no husband. Jesus said unto her, Thou hast well said, I have no husband: For thou hast had five husbands; and he whom thou now hast is not thy husband: in that saidst thou truly," —John 4:17-18. (See also Acts 9:11).

Faith

The ability to believe God without human reasoning:

"And Peter answered him and said, Lord, if it be thou, bid me come unto thee on the water. And he said, Come. And when Peter was come down out of the ship, he walked on the water, to go to Jesus," —Matthew 14:28. (See also Hebrews 11:6).

Healing

The power to heal all kinds of illnesses without human intervention:

"And he commanded the multitude to sit down on the grass, and took the five loaves, and the two fishes, and looking up to heaven, he blessed, and brake, and gave the loaves to his disciples, and the disciples to the multitude. And they did all eat, and were filled: and they took up of the fragments that remained twelve baskets full. And they that had eaten were about five thousand men, beside women and children." —Matthew 14:19-21

Prophecy

Speaking to teach, persuade, and comfort:

"Hear ye now what the Lord saith; Arise, contend thou before the mountains, and let the hills hear thy voice. Hear ye, O mountains, the Lord's controversy, and ye strong foundations of the earth: for the Lord hath a controversy with his people, and he will plead with Israel." —Micah 6:1-2

Discerning of Spirits

Knowing if a spirit is good or evil, including knowing others' thoughts and intentions:

"And Jesus knew their thoughts, and said unto them, 'Every kingdom divided against itself is brought to desolation; and every city or house divided against itself shall not stand.'" —Matthew 12:25.

Speaking in Tongues

Speaking in strange languages while in prayer:

"If any man speak in an unknown tongue, let it be by two, or at the most by three, and that by course; and let one interpret." —1 Corinthians 14:27:

Interpretation of Tongues

The ability to interpret what is spoken in other tongues that are unknown by the interpreter:

"But if there be no interpreter, let him keep silence in the church; and let him speak to himself, and to God." —1 Corinthians 14:28:

Be open to the Holy Spirit so that He can use you whenever the need arises. It is God's will that all men who need the gifts receive them, but He can only do it through you. The Spirit wills—do you?

BE EVER-FILLED

"But he that is joined unto the Lord is one spirit," —1 Corinthians 6:17. We are one with the Father, Son, and Holy Spirit. The real you is the spirit in you. Now your spirit is joined with the Holy Spirit and you are one with Him. Just as Jesus and the Father are one; so, too, are we. The real God the Father, and the real Jesus the Son, are spirits. They put their spirit into us to make us one with them. Both Jesus and the Father love and reverence the Holy Spirit. How much more should we? Don't be afraid of putting too much honor on the Holy Spirit—He is God. How much should God be reverenced and honored? With all that we are, with all our heart, mind and soul. The Holy Spirit is more than a power, He's more than the Father's helper, and He's more than tongues—He's the Almighty Being of God living in us.

The first time we see the Holy Spirit in the Bible is in Genesis 1:2: *"And the earth was without form, and void; and darkness was upon the face of the deep. And the Spirit of God moved upon the face of the waters."* The Hebrew word describing the Holy Spirit is "ruach," meaning breath or soul, the life force. In Greek, the word "pneuma" means, "the same, for where there is breath, there is life." So we see the breath of God, a mighty wind, blowing across the waters. "Then God said, 'Let there be light: and there was light.'" As the Father spoke, "Let there be light," the Holy Spirit went forth and accomplished it.

In the New Testament, the Holy Spirit hovered over Mary, breathing upon her, making her ready to bring forth life. When she received the Word of God, she conceived Jesus, the Son. The Holy Spirit later hovered over Jesus at His baptism to make Him ready to bring forth life.

Nowadays, the Holy Spirit hovers over believers that ask Him, making us ready to bring forth life and accomplish the words of God. Just as the mantle of Elijah fell upon Elisha and he received a double portion (or double anointing), so the mantle of Jesus has fallen upon His body. Not as a coat, but as the Holy Spirit! That's why Jesus said, *"Verily, verily, I say unto you, He that believeth on me, the works that I do shall he do also; and greater works than these shall he do; because I go unto my Father,"* —John 14:12. What happened when He went to the Father? He sent the Holy Spirit. Let Him come upon you, and receive the ability to do greater works than Jesus!

Ephesians 5:18 says, *"And be not drunk with wine, wherein is excess; but be filled with the Spirit."* In Acts Chapter 2, we saw the 120 get filled with the Holy Spirit. Peter (who was so weak in his own strength) got filled, preached, and thousands came to Jesus after his very first sermon. Why? Because Peter became a brand new man!

In Acts Chapter 4, Peter and John were arrested and com-

manded by the law to stop preaching in "that name." The believers began to pray: *"And when they had prayed, the place was shaken
where they were assembled together; and they were all filled with the
Holy Ghost, and they spake the word of God with boldness. And the
multitude of them that believed were of one heart and of one soul: neither said any of them that ought of the things which he possessed was his
own; but they had all things common,"* —Acts 4:31-32.

Note in verse 31 it said they were filled with the Holy Spirit.
Now, wait a minute—I thought they were filled in Acts, Chapter
2! You see, when we receive Jesus as Lord, it's a one-time experience. We don't need to continually receive Him over and over.
Brand new Christians are notorious for going up to every altar
call to receive Jesus in their heart. Finally, when they are taught
that Jesus came in and will not leave them, they relax and just
enjoy His presence. Sometimes we think that if we were baptized
in the Holy Spirit ten years ago, the Holy Spirit is a one-time experience. But we must be ever-filled with the Holy Spirit.

Look what happens in the Bible when men are ever-filled
with the Holy Spirit. We saw in Acts 4:31 that they were filled
and spoke the word with boldness. When you are ever-filled,
you will be bold in the word!

Stephen was being stoned to death for preaching the Gospel
of Truth. Instead of feeling the pain and being filled with fear, he
was filled with the Holy Ghost—and he saw the Father and the

Son in heaven! *"But he, being full of the Holy Ghost, looked up stead-fastly into heaven, and saw the glory of God, and Jesus standing on the right hand of God,"* —Acts 7:55. When we are ever-filled, we won't be in fear. We won't feel the pain of our circumstances. We'll see the glory of God!

"Then Saul, (who also is called Paul,) filled with the Holy Ghost, set his eyes on him. And said, O full of all subtlety and all mischief, thou child of the devil, thou enemy of all righteousness, wilt thou not cease to pervert the right ways of the Lord?" —Acts 13:9-10.

Can you imagine calling someone a devil? When we are ever-filled with the Spirit, we will speak the truth. We are commanded to be ever-filled. The Bible tells us not to be drunk with wine, but be ever-filled with the Holy Spirit. Just like wine is intoxicating, so is the Holy Spirit. Wine controls the drinker, and the Holy Spirit controls the partaker. We must continue to be filled with the Holy Spirit, just like a drunk must drink often to stay drunk. If the drunk doesn't continue drinking, he will dry out. If we don't continue to partake of the Holy Spirit, we will dry out, too. Galatians 5:16 lays it out there pretty clear, *"This I say then, walk in the Spirit, and ye shall not fulfill the lust of the flesh."* Also, *"if we live in the Spirit, let us also walk in the Spirit,"* —Galatians 5:25.

WALK IN THE SPIRIT

We are told to walk in the Spirit. We can do this because He's bigger than us. When He moves, we must move. If we are not moving when He moves, we are not walking in Him. We must live in Him. We are not our own, our lives are with the Holy Spirit. The Bible says for us to live is Christ (Philippians 1:21). It also says that we are living the life of the Spirit. The very life of the Spirit is lived by us. *"For as many as are led by the Spirit of God, they are the sons of God,"* —Romans 8:14.

He must lead us. Where He moves, we must move. We must stay that close to Him. I was driving my car the other day and my mind was busy going through all the events of the upcoming week. Hours went by, and I realized that I couldn't sense the presence of the Holy Spirit. For months, He had been my constant companion and now I didn't know where He was. I called out to Him, but nothing seemed to change. When I got home, I opened my Bible and saw that the Holy Spirit was my Helper, so I called upon the Helper to help me know and understand what I had done.

The Holy Spirit spoke and said, "Claudia, I've been with you in the car all day, and you ignored me the whole time. If one of your friends was with you, you would have talked the entire time. I want a relationship with you." I apologized, and vowed to be more sensitive to Him. I realized how hurt the Holy Spirit can get. He is the sensitive part of the Godhead.

Jesus was very protective of the Holy Spirit. Matthew 12:31 and 32 expresses it well, *"Wherefore I say unto you, all manner of sin and blasphemy shall be forgiven unto men: but the blasphemy against the Holy Ghost shall not be forgiven unto men. And whosoever speaketh a word against the Son of man, it shall be forgiven him: but whosoever speaketh against the Holy Ghost, it shall not be forgiven him, neither in this world, neither in the world to come."*

The Holy Spirit also gets outraged. Hebrews 10:29 asks, *"Of how much sorer punishment, suppose ye, shall he be thought worthy, who hath trodden under foot the Son of God, and hath counted the blood of the covenant, wherewith he was sanctified, an unholy thing, and hath done despite unto the Spirit of grace?"*

In Isaiah 63:10, the prophet gives account of the time Israel when *" . . . they rebelled, and vexed his Holy Spirit: therefore he was turned to be their enemy, and he fought against them."*

Ananias and his wife Sapphira lied about their donation: *"But Peter said, Ananias, why hath Satan filled thine heart to lie to the Holy Ghost, and to keep back part of the price of the land?"* —Acts 5:3. And Ananias fell dead!

The Bible clearly warns that we should not grieve or distress the Holy Spirit (Ephesians 4:30). When we are in trouble and we don't rely on the Holy Spirit as our Helper, we grieve Him by not allowing Him to fulfill His ministry. 1 Thessalonians 5:19 clearly states, *"Quench not the Spirit,"* or "put the light out—to stop inspiration." Many churches start out with the Holy Spirit ruling over their services, but then their "programs" become very important. You hear a man's plans, but how often do you hear, "The Holy Spirit says that this is what we are to do?" In Acts, every time there was a supernatural word coming forth, it says, "Thus says the Holy Spirit . . ."

In the Book of Revelation, it is the Holy Spirit speaking to the churches. Many churches that started with the Holy Spirit in leadership are now nothing more than tombs with dead men's bones, because they stopped being ever-filled. If a church was once led by the Holy Spirit but is no longer, His leading is usually replaced with legalism, ritual, and religion. The law is now their guide, but the law brings death. It's the Holy Spirit that brings life.

Paul was led by the Spirit. He communed with Him and was in fellowship with Him. Acts 15:28 is a witness, *"For it seemed good to the Holy Ghost, and to us, to lay upon you no greater burden than these necessary things."* As it seemed good to the person of the Holy Spirit, it was also to his partner Paul. As Paul traveled, the Holy Spirit twice forbade Paul to go to a certain place. But one time a man came with a word from the Holy Spirit for Paul: *"And when he was come unto us, he took Paul's girdle, and bound his own hands and feet, and said, Thus saith the Holy Ghost, So shall the Jews at Jerusalem bind the man that owneth this girdle, and shall deliv-*

er him into the hands of the Gentiles," —Acts 21:11.

Now, some people say if Paul had listened to the Holy Spirit, he wouldn't have died, but Paul knew the Holy Spirit well. The Holy Spirit had twice before forbidden him to go to certain places, but now the Holy Spirit didn't forbid Paul, He simply told him of his situation. Paul knew full well what would happen and yet, he still chose to go. *"Then Paul answered, 'What mean ye to weep and to break mine heart? For I am ready not to be bound only, but also to die at Jerusalem for the name of the Lord Jesus,'"* —Acts 21:13. The Holy Spirit will always warn us ahead of time. He can be trusted.

THE FRUIT OF THE HOLY SPIRIT

"But the fruit of the Spirit is love, joy, peace, long suffering, gentleness, goodness, faith, Meekness, temperance: against such there is no law," —Galatians 5:22-23. This is the fruit of the Spirit, not of ourselves. His presence within us accomplishes the following things in our lives:

Love
The Greek word is "agape," divine love, a strong unconditional, tender, compassionate devotion. There is no way human love can compare to the God kind of love. We in and of ourselves at best can only have a condition-

al love. Human love is often selfish, while the love of the Spirit is shown in 1 Corinthians 13. When we feel that we cannot love, we need to rely on the Holy Spirit and let Him love through us. Romans, Chapter 5 tells us that the love of God has been shed abroad in our hearts by the Holy Spirit.

Joy

The Greek word is "chara," meaning "delight, over a blessing received or expected." Even when our circumstances don't line up with the Word of God, we can be in joy because we know the end result. We win! Jesus, for the joy that was set before Him, endured the cross. He didn't have delight over the trial, but He saw us—the joy—and went through the cross. When we need joy, draw from the Spirit of Joy!

Peace

In Greek, "eirene." It means "the state of quietness, repose, harmony, order in the midst of strife and trials." Paul was in perfect peace while in prison because he knew the Spirit of Peace.

Longsuffering

The Greek word is "mabrothumia," which means "patient endurance; to bear with offenses without resentment." On our own, we can't help but take offense to a wrong done to us. But Jesus was our example in long suffering when He was on the cross. He said, "Father, forgive them, for they know not what they do." The Holy Spirit is the Spirit of Patience. He is in us, and we can give out His fruit.

Gentleness

In Greek, "agathosume," meaning "the state of being good, generous in life and conduct." This is consistently being like God, the Good Spirit. He is consistent.

Faith

The Greek word is "pistis," or "the living divinely implanted principle of assurance and reliance on God and all that He says." The Holy Spirit is the Spirit of Faith. We may try to get faith, but we already have it because we have the Spirit of Faith.

Meekness

In Greek, "praotes." It means, "even balance in temper and passions."

Temperance

The Greek word is "embraleia," meaning "self-control, a moderation in indulgence." I'm glad to know that the fruit of the Holy Spirit is self-control. I don't have control in my flesh, but the Holy Spirit is my self-control.

Let me impart to you the revelation on the fruit of the Holy Spirit that was given to me. Fruit, in the natural world, such as an apple, is good for our bodies. When we give an apple to someone, it nourishes them. But contained in that apple is reproductive seed, so it can reproduce apples. The fruit of the Holy Spirit is the same—not only do people partake of the fruit of love that we give out, but they receive the seeds to reproduce it in their own lives. If you see someone without joy, give them the Holy Spirit fruit of Joy to them. It will be contagious! Not only will they receive the joy, but they will have the ability to give it to others. Let His presence within you produce the fruit. You are the branches, rooted in the vine, which is Jesus—with fruit from the Holy Spirit to offer.

NAMES OF THE GODHEAD

In Genesis 1:26, we hear God talking about man's creation and his dominion, *"And God said, Let us make man in our image, after our likeness: and let them have dominion over the fish of the sea, and over the fowl of the air, and over the cattle, and over all the earth, and over every creeping thing that creepeth upon the earth."* Notice that it was God the Father, God the Son, and God the Holy Spirit that man was made in the likeness of. So when we see the image that we were made after, we must see not only the Father, but also the

Son and the Holy Spirit.

When we learn the meanings of the names of the Father, we find out the aspects of His character. **"Jehovah Jireh"** (Gen. 22:14), tells us The Lord Provides. **"Jehovah Nissi"** (Exodus 17:15), The Lord is My Banner, is always overshadowing us, just as His name indicates. He's also called **"Jehovah Shalom"** (Judges 6:24), the Lord Sends Peace. **"Jehovah Shammah,"** (Ezekiel 48:35) means The Lord is There, reminding us of His continual presence. **"Jehovah Tsidkenu"** (Jer. 23:6) is The Lord our Righteousness—and He is our righteousness, just as His name says He is. The character is contained within the name.

As we study the names of the Father, Son, and Holy Spirit, we will see the image we've been created after. When we pray in the name of Jesus, we are praying in all that His name contains. He is called our **Advocate** (1 John 2:1), the **Chief Shepherd** (1 Peter 5:4), **Counselor** (Isaiah 9:6), **Deliverer** (Romans 11:26), **First and Last** (Revelation 1:17), **Immanuel** (Isaiah 7:14), and the **Most High** (Deuteronomy 32:8). He is called many other names. When you call on the name of Jesus, every name that is His is yours. You are praying in the name of the Shepherd, Deliverer, Healer, or whatever you need. His name is His character.

As I was looking up the names of Jesus, I noticed that Satan had names, too. (I thought he would be called "dog" or "pig," but he really has names.) The Bible says that Jesus has the name above every name (Philippians 2:9), so I've listed the titles of Satan and the titles of Jesus. Jesus' Name is greater than Satan's!

SATAN'S NAMES	JESUS' NAMES
Accuser (Rev. 12:10)	**Advocate (1 John 2:1)**
Adversary (1 Peter 5:8)	**Father and Friend (Acts 10:36)**
God of this world (2 Cor.4:4)	**Almighty Lord of All (John 11:25)**
Murderer (John 8:44)	**Resurrection (John 11:25)**
Prince of the Power of the Air (Eph. 2:2)	**Most High (Deut. 32:8)**
Ruler of Darkness (Eph. 6:12)	**Light of the World (John 8:12)**
Tempter (Matt. 4:3)	**Fortress (2 Sam. 2:22)**
Unclean Spirit (Matt. 12:43)	**Holy One (Acts 3:14)**
Wicked One (Matt. 13:19)	**The Just One (Acts 7:52)**
Prince of Devils (Matt. 12:24)	**King of Kings (1 Tim. 6:15)**

Notice that in each instance, Jesus has the Name that invalidates the name of Satan—every time, all the time!

The Holy Spirit also has names, which reveal His character as well:

Spirit of God (Genesis 1:2)

Spirit of Grace (Zechariah 12:10)

Free Spirit (Psalm 51:12)

Holy Spirit (Psalm 51:11)

Spirit of wisdom, counsel, might, and fear of the Lord (Isaiah 11:2)

Spirit of the Lord (Isaiah 61:6)

Spirit of Judgment (Isaiah 4:4)

Comforter (John 14:6)

Spirit of the Father (Matthew 10:20)

Spirit of Adoption (Romans 8:15)

Spirit of Faith (2 Corinthians 4:13)

Spirit of Life (Romans 8:10)

Spirit of Adoption (Romans 8:15)

Spirit of Glory (1 Peter 4:4)

Spirit of Peace and Joy (Romans 14:17)

Spirit of Truth (John 14:17)

Spirit of Righteousness (Romans 8:10)

Eternal Spirit (Hebrews 9:14)

Spirit of Prophecy (Revelation 19:10)

These are *some* of the names of the Holy Spirit. Through His Name, we can grasp hold of His character. I want to point out that the Holy Spirit is given to us as a gift from God. As we discover His character, we will get to know our gift. He is called the Comforter because He knows all things about our hearts as well as the Father's heart. He is able to give us the answers we need. When He comes inside us, all things that are His now belong to us because we are His temple—we are one. Read 2 Corinthians 6:16: *"And what agreement hath the temple of God with idols? For ye are the temple of the living God; as God hath said, I will dwell in them, and walk in them; and I will be their God, and they shall be my people."* We are one spirit with God and He dwells in us.

The Body of Christ has been crying out for miracles. The only way consistent miracles of God can happen is through the Holy Spirit. If we are one with the Holy Spirit, and He is allowed to be free, then we will see miracles. Every miracle in the Bible was done by the Holy Spirit, through man—but man can't do it alone. We need the Holy Spirit to take control.

We need to know the Holy Spirit's attributes so that we can know Him. The last thing Jesus told the disciples as He ascended was to go out to all the world and preach, baptizing them into the name of the Father, and the Son, and the Holy Spirit (Matthew 28:18). Remember that the word "baptize" means, "immerse, to fully cover." He was saying, "As you go, preach—immerse them in the name of the Father, immerse them in the name of the Son, immerse them in the name of the Holy Spirit. This is our commission, so let's go for it!

I've listed some symbols that represent the Holy Spirit in the Bible. Each symbol includes the Holy Spirit's character. Please read each and look up the scripture examples:

Bird or Dove
Symbols of meekness and humility, (Genesis 8:8-11 and Luke 3:22).

Wind
Cleanses the air; no one can be in control of it—continuous motion. (John 3:8).

Fire
Refines, gives light, and symbolizes power, (Acts 2:3, Matthew 3:11 and Hebrews 12:29).

Water
Cleanses, purifies, and sustains life, (John 7:38 and Titus 3:5).

Wine
It controls you—but to stay intoxicated, you must keep drinking! (Ephesians 5:18 and Acts 2:12, 13).

Oil
Used to easily move or motivate, to set apart, (I Sam 16:13 and 1 John 2:27).

Rain
Grows and sustains vegetation on the earth, (Hosea 6:3 and Joel 2:23).

THESE THREE AGREE

"This is he that came by water and blood, even Jesus Christ; not by water only, but by water and blood. And it is the Spirit that beareth witness, because the Spirit is truth. For there are three that bear record in heaven, the Father, the Word, and the Holy Ghost: and these three are one. And there are three that bear witness in earth, the Spirit, and the water, and the blood: and these three agree in one," —I John 5:6-8.

This passage of scripture is somewhat confusing at first glance, but as we study it, I believe "the light will shine." The term "trinity" is never used in the Bible, but a word meaning the same thing, "Godhead," is used. Godhead simply defined means God the Father, God the Son, and God the Holy Spirit. They are one and in unity, yet separate in person.

Refer to Genesis 1:26-28: *"And God said, Let us make man in our image, after our likeness: and let them have dominion over the fish of the sea, and over the fowl of the air, and over the cattle, and over all the earth, and over every creeping thing that creepeth upon the earth.*

"So God created man in his own image, in the image of God creat-ed he him; male and female created he them.

"And God blessed them, and God said unto them, Be fruitful, and multiply, and replenish the earth, and subdue it: and have dominion over the fish of the sea, and over the fowl of the air, and over every living thing that moveth upon the earth."

So we are made in Their image. The word "one" means "in unity," (John 17:11, 21-23). There is one God the Father, one Lord Jesus Christ, and one Holy Spirit (1 Corinthians 8:6). Ephesians 4:3-6 says that all three are distinct persons. They are all called by individual names, and they are all called God at times. God the Father is called God in 1 Corinthians 8:6: "But to us there is but one God, the Father, of whom are all things, and we in him; and one Lord Jesus Christ, by whom are all things, and we by him."

God the Son is called God in Isaiah 9:6-7: *"For unto us a child is born, unto us a son is given: and the government shall be upon his shoulder: and his name shall be called Wonderful, Counselor, the Mighty God, the Everlasting Father, the Prince of Peace. Of the increase of his government and peace there shall be no end, upon the throne of David, and upon his kingdom, to order it, and to establish it with judgment and with justice from henceforth-even forever. The zeal of the Lord of hosts will perform this."*

The Holy Spirit is called God in Acts 5:3-4: *"But Peter said, Ananias, why hath Satan filled thine heart to lie to the Holy Ghost, and to keep back part of the price of the land? Whiles it remained, was it not thine own? And after it was sold, was it not in thine own power? Why hast thou conceived this thing in thine heart? Thou hast not lied unto men, but unto God."*

The term "God" can be used is singular form or in plural form. When used singularly, we see their different offices or positions. When used in its plural form, it can refer to any two persons of the Godhead, or all three. Many times the Godhead is seen by man, together. This proves that there are three beings. *"And Jesus, when he was baptized, went up straightway out of the water: and, lo, the heavens were opened unto him, and he saw the Spirit of God descending like a dove, and lighting upon him,"* —Matthew 3:16.

We see all the members of the Godhead mentioned separately here, and yet in unity. These are three distinct, separate witnesses that bear witness of Christ. It is a Biblical requirement that any word must be confirmed by two or more witnesses: *"But if he will not hear thee, then take with thee one or two more, that in the mouth of two or three witnesses every word may be established,"* —Matthew 18:16.

Furthermore, 2 Corinthians 13:1 affirms, *"This is the third time I am coming to you. In the mouth of two or three witnesses shall every word be established."* Therefore, we must have at least two witnesses concerning Christ. In Matthew 3:16, we find three witnesses in the testimonies of the Father, Son, and Holy Spirit—the three testimonies alone are enough to establish the truth that Jesus is the Son of God.

THE WATER & THE BLOOD

The water and the blood confirm their testimonies. You see, when Jesus was baptized in water, representing His death, burial, and resurrection, the Holy Spirit came and bore witness of it. The blood was shed to redeem us from sin. The blood and the water both flowed at His death, testifying of His humanity. John 19:34 reports, *"But one of the soldiers with a spear pierced his side, and forthwith came there out blood and water."*

The similarities between blood and the Holy Spirit are amazing. As I realized that the Spirit and the blood agree in reference to Jesus, these similarities became more important to me, so let me share a few of them with you. Romans 5:9 says that we are justified by the blood. We're made as though we had never sinned. But 1 Timothy 3:16 says that we are justified in Spirit!

Hebrews 13:12 declares that it is the blood that sanctifies us, but 2 Thessalonians 2:13 says that the Holy Spirit is our sanctification. In Colossians 1:20, Jesus made peace through His blood. But in Romans 14:17, it's the Holy Spirit who brings peace and joy. The Holy Spirit and the blood bear witness together concerning the work of salvation.

So we see that there are three distinct persons who bear witness in heaven: the Father, the Son (the Word), and the Holy Spirit. On earth, the witnesses are the Spirit, the baptism (water), and the redeeming blood. All of them testify of the same thing—salvation through the Son. I have drawn-up a chart to show the similar functions of the Godhead. Although the dispensations of their ministry are different, they all have the same purpose:

FUNCTIONS OF THE GODHEAD

FATHER	**JESUS**	**HOLY SPIRIT**
Taught	Taught in Temple	Will teach you
(John 8:28)	(Luke 19:47)	(John 14:26)
Will never leave us	I will never leave you	Will remain forever
(John 10:36)	(Hebrews 13:5)	(John 14:16)
Sanctifies us	I sanctify Myself so that	Sanctified by the
(John 10:36)	you may be sanctified	Holy Spirit
	(Romans 15:16)	(John 17:19)

FATHER	**JESUS**	**HOLY SPIRIT**
Holy Father (John 17:11)	Holy One of God (Luke 4:34)	Holy Spirit (Psalm 51:11)
Father of Glory (Ephesians 1:17)	Behold Jesus' glory (John 1:14)	Spirit of Glory (1 Peter 4:14)
Make our abode in you (John 14:23)	Make our abode in you (John 14:23)	Made abode on Jesus (John 1:32)
Father of Truth (2 John 3)	I Am the Truth (John 14:6)	Spirit of Truth (Isaiah 11:2)
Father of Light (James 1:17)	I have come as a Light (John 12:46)	Tongues like fire (Acts 2:3)
Father has life in Himself (John 5:25)	I Am the Life (John 14:6)	Spirit of Life (Romans 8:2)
God is Wisdom (Job 36:5)	Christ is Wisdom (1 Corinthians 1:24)	Spirit of Wisdom (Exodus 28:3)
God of Knowledge (1 Samuel 2:3)	Knowledge of Christ (Philippians 3:8)	Spirit of Knowledge (James 11:2)
Word was God and Life (John 1:1)	Word became flesh (John 1:14)	Words are Spirit (John 6:63)
	Jesus our advocate with the Father (1 John 2:1)	Holy Spirit is called advocate (John 15:16)

These three agree!

RELATIONSHIP WITH ONE ANOTHER

"And I will pray the Father, and he shall give you another Comforter, that he may abide with you for ever; Even the Spirit of truth; whom the world cannot receive, because it seeth him not, neither knoweth him: but ye know him; for he dwelleth with you, and shall be in you," —John 14:16-17.

I want to point out an interesting word here—the word "another." There are two Greek words used for our English word "another." One definition is "one of the same kind," while the other definition means "one of a different kind." In this passage, Jesus uses both Greek words. He says, "I'm sending one of the same kind and of a different kind." In other words, the Holy Spirit is going to be just like Jesus—and different.

Keep in mind the events, which were happening in John, chapter 14. The disciples had walked away from their jobs, their families, and all they owned so they could follow Jesus. As Jesus told them He was leaving, and that He would send the Holy Spirit, I'm sure that fear gripped their hearts. That's why Jesus told them in John 16:7, Nevertheless I tell you the truth; It is expedient for you that I go away: for if I go not away, the Comforter will not come unto you; but if I depart, I will send him unto you." Jesus was explaining to the disciples that the exact relationship they now had with Him, they would soon have with the Holy Spirit.

You see they depended on Jesus for their every need. They

looked to Jesus for their direction. And now, Jesus was going away—but He did not leave them helpless. He gave them far more in the Holy Spirit than they ever had with Him. Jesus was limited by His physical body, so he could only be at one place at a time. But now, the Holy Spirit would come, having no physical limitations. He could be with Christians in Africa and in the United States at the same time.

Jesus said the Holy Spirit would be in close fellowship with us. The Holy Spirit wants to be closer than the closest friend. He wants an intimate relationship. This is not a temporary relationship, but a permanent one (James 4:5). Jesus said He will remain with you forever. And forever is a long, long time! Now is a good time to get to know our permanent friend. 2 Corinthians 13:14 says, *"The grace of the Lord Jesus Christ, and the love of God, and the communion of the Holy Ghost, be with you all. Amen."* Fellowship of the Spirit, fellowship with believers—to commune with us.

One of His names is "Stand-by." He will be along side us, giving us power, might and ability. He is our permanent Helper with a residency in our hearts, standing by to render instant help. We can't have relationship with a power, but we can have relationship with the person of the Holy Spirit. In relationships, we get to know the other person. When you begin a relationship, you're filled with questions. You share your views—you share your feelings.

When I first received the baptism of the Holy Spirit and spoke in tongues, I felt incredible! For weeks, I could hear the voice of the Spirit in clarity. I received exact direction from Him. During this time, I saw a vision of my friend in the hospital—so I drove there. Sure enough, she had just arrived. I was able to see her as she was healed.

Not long afterward, the Spirit told me to drive to a certain intersection, and that I would see a girl there. I knew that I was supposed to pick her up and tell her about Jesus. He told me she would receive Him. I drove to that corner, and Karen was there. I picked her up and told her about Jesus. She got out of my car, told me "where to go," and slammed my door. I didn't see her again, so I was confused—it didn't seem to have happened as I was told it would.

Ten years later—that's right, exactly ten years—I got a phone call from Karen. She asked me if I was still a Christian. I said, "Oh yes, and now I'm a minister for Jesus Christ." She began to cry. She told me that when I preached to her ten years earlier, she got out of my car and told God, "If You're for real, Claudia will still be a Christian in ten years. And if she is, I will become a Christian. If she is not still serving You, then neither will I!" Praise God for His keeping power. I'm so glad I still walk with Jesus! Karen received Jesus that very day—ten years later!

I told you these stories so that you could see how clearly the

Holy Spirit wants to speak to us. But as months went by, I didn't hear so clearly. Soon years went by. I'd spoken in tongues daily since I was baptized years ago, but I once came to a point where had lost fellowship. I asked the Holy Spirit, "What happened? How did I stop hearing you clearly for so many years?" He told me that I had stopped listening! I've heard people say that the Holy Spirit is a gentleman. I've never liked that term, because I thought it wasn't scriptural. But the Holy Spirit said, "Claudia, I am a gentleman. I will not push my ways on you. I will tell you which way to go, but if you don't, I will stand back from you until you call me." So, I did. And, in spite of the time that had passed, I found a new and greater communion with the Holy Spirit.

You see the Holy Spirit wants us to willingly submit to His authority. But we must ask the Holy Spirit to come, to be our Helper and Teacher. The Holy Spirit comes inside the believer when we are baptized in Him. But He wants to come upon us so that we are totally immersed in Him. He wants to be inside and outside. You must ask Him to come upon you. John said, "There is coming One who will baptize you with the Holy Spirit and with fire." Many Christians have been baptized with the Holy Spirit and have spoken in other tongues, but few Christians have been baptized with fire. The Holy Spirit wants to baptize you in fire—He wants to consume you—let Him! Call upon Him to come and take control of your life. ❀

PART V

PICTURES OF THE HEART

"As a man thinketh in his heart, so is he!"

Proiverbs 23:7

PICTURES OF THE HEART

I have a foundational teaching on this scripture that I know will change your life. When I was in prayer before the Father, He began to reveal the importance of this scripture to me by giving me the illustration I'm about to share with you. It has changed the way I look at things. It's changed my entire ministry!

As I was in prayer, God said this to me (and yes, the Father—and the Holy Spirit—and Jesus—do speak!). He said to me, "If I gave you a piece of paper, and told you to draw a person you'd like to look like, who would you draw?"

I thought about it for a while, and I said, "I know—I'll draw a picture of one of the most beautiful people I've ever met—I'll draw Cheryl Salem, the former Miss America, a very beautiful woman."

God asked, "Why wouldn't you draw somebody ugly on that paper?"

I replied, "Because I wouldn't want to become somebody ugly—I'd want to become somebody very beautiful!"

And He said, "Yet My Word, which is absolute fact and absolute authority, has said, 'As you think in your heart, so you are.' Yet you allow thoughts in your mind that are not from Me. You allow ugliness in your heart that is not from Me. My word is truth, and it says, 'As you think in your heart so you are.'"

Now I ask you—if God gave you a piece of paper and said, "You draw anyone on that paper and you'll become that person," who would you draw? Of course, I hope you'd draw someone beautiful. Then realize that as you think in your heart, so you are.

The Spirit spoke again and said, "If I gave you a piece of paper and told you that whatever dollar amount you wrote on that paper you would have, what figure would you write?"

I said, "I'd write a 'one' with as many zeroes after it as I could fit on that page." If God gave you a piece of paper and said, "write in any dollar amount and you'll have it," what would you write? My husband says he'd write as many nines as he could fit on the paper!

After I decided on my dollar figure, the Holy Spirit said, "Why didn't you put a minus sign before the dollar amount?"

I replied, "I don't want to owe that amount of money, I want to have that amount of money!"

Once again He stressed, "Yet my Word, that is absolute fact and absolute authority, has said 'As you think in your heart so you are.' You've allowed a poverty mentality and fear into your heart, and you're becoming what you think."

CONFESSION ALONE IS NOT ENOUGH

You see my mouth was under control. I had trained it in the Word. When problems came, or bills that I couldn't pay came in, I'd say, *"But my God shall supply all your need according to his riches in glory by Christ Jesus,"* —Philippians 4:19. But inside, my heart was in a total panic. My mouth quoted a scripture and said all the right words, but my heart said, "Oh, no—not another bill! How are we going to ever pay it? I hate this, I hate the pressure!" I had total fear.

You see, I'd been taught for so long that the confessions of our mouth are what we live by—and there's truth in that. I believe in confession, and I teach it, but there's more to confession than just "lip service." The Bible tells us "out of the abundance of the heart, the mouth speaks." We've been trying to get our mouths to speak correctly, instead of working on our hearts. We must get our hearts in line with the Word of God, and then our mouths would speak correct truths. Did you know that you can speak correct things, yet in your heart really believe the wrong things? But if, in your heart, you believe the right things, your mouth will soon line up.

GOD LOOKS AT THE HEART

In my heart I had put ugly pictures. When I would not perform in an area up to my capacity, I would begin to condemn myself, thinking, "You're always this way, never doing things right."
I would begin to put images of failure in my heart, and confirm
other wrong images. This process would cause me to transform
into the images in my heart. There have been successful people
throughout history, and I guarantee you that before they achieved
success, they saw it in their hearts—an image of success—before
they ever succeeded. The man who lives on the streets in failure
saw himself as a failure long before he ever became one. It's so
important how we view ourselves in our hearts.

Jesus understood this very well. He was the Word of God,
and He could place images inside people's hearts continually. In
Matthew 5:2 Jesus teaches, *"And he opened his mouth, and taught
them, saying, 'Blessed are the poor in spirit: for theirs is the kingdom of
heaven. Blessed are they that mourn: for they shall be comforted. Blessed are the meek: for they shall inherit the earth. Blessed are they which
do hunger and thirst after righteousness: for they shall be filled. Blessed
are the merciful: for they shall obtain mercy. Blessed are the pure in
heart: for they shall see God. Blessed are the peacemakers: for they shall
be called the children of God. Blessed are they which are persecuted for*

righteousness' sake: for theirs is the kingdom of heaven.'"

Jesus was looking out to a crowd of people who were poor physically, spiritually, and mentally. Yet He said, "Blessed are you!" He spoke forth a life-changing picture to them.

God the Father looked at Abraham and said, "I no longer call you Abram, but Abraham—father of multitudes." God knew that Abraham and Sarah's bodies were too old to have children, but God called him a new name. God is a faith God. He knows that as a man thinks, so is he, so He had to put a new image inside Abraham: "You are a father of multitudes. Get the new picture in your heart, Abraham!"

FAITH IS A SUBSTANCE

We understand that faith is the substance of things hoped for (Hebrews 11:1). It's not some strange force that we can't get a hold of. It's not that "sometimes we have it, sometimes we don't." Faith is a substance, just as wood is a substance, and clay. In the spirit, faith is tangible, like wood and clay is tangible in the physical. Simply put, faith is the picture we have inside our hearts. Poor picture—poor faith. Correct picture (according to the Word)—great faith. Just as wood is a substance that is used to make desks, pencils, and other things, faith is a substance, which God uses to make our blessings. To God, releasing faith in line with His Word is like giving wood to a builder.

If we give incomplete pictures—partial faith—then we've given inadequate supplies to the builder and we get partial answers from God. He wants us to have complete faith, so we can have complete answers.

RIGHT & WRONG PICTURES

When we built the inside of our tour bus, we had drafting plans. The builder went by the drafting plans, and if we needed changes, we had to get new ones. If we had given the builder incomplete drafting plans, we would have had an incomplete bus.

Faith is the drafting plans for our today, as well as our future. As we draft our plans according to the Spirit, in line with His Word, then the Word of God becomes a description of our todays and tomorrows. The trick of the enemy is to produce "negative" images in our hearts through lies. When you have photographs developed, you not only get the pictures, but the negatives also. When you hold the negative to the light, whatever is light appears dark, and whatever is dark appears light. It's the exact opposite of reality.

Now faith is the "picture" of things hoped for. If you have the correct picture in your heart of who Christ says you are, you have great faith. If you have a wrong picture in your heart, such as, "I'm a failure," then you may see yourself failing in any and every area of life. But that wrong picture is opposite to the Word of God, Who says in His Word that He's already perfected you (Hebrews 10:14). According to the Word of God, He has put His seal of approval on you. But in your heart you see yourself as disappointing to God and to your own expectations. What has happened? You've allowed negative pictures to enter and live on in your heart, and that negative in your heart is not producing Godly faith. But when the light of His Word comes in, it passes through the negative, producing the correct picture. As you read these words, pictures are being created in you from the Father, through this book to you.

Satan tries to put images in our heads—maybe a picture of our children being hurt, or of divorce, pictures of fear, failure or any other manner of evil. He wants to put pictures in your mind, hoping that you'll meditate on the negative until it gets down into your heart. That produces the opposite of what faith in God's Word produces.

What you think you are, you will be. Accordingly, you will become what others say you are, if you entertain their words. We hear parents say, "Oh, he's going to be a bum, he'll never make it." Then when the child grows up—surprise, surprise—he's a bum, and he can't make it! On the other side, some parents continually speak over their children saying, "You're so smart, so obedient and nice!" The child grows up smart, obedient and full of confidence. They have fulfilled that which was spoken over them.

Pictures are being created as you read and receive these words. In church services, I have found that whatever subject a minister preaches on is what the congregation receives in their hearts—no surprise there! If I preach on salvation, the altar call is anointed for salvations. But if I preach on tithing, and then I have an altar call for receiving the infilling the Holy Spirit, I'm almost fighting myself—and the Spirit—because as I preached, certain specific images were in the hearts of the hearers.

Actually, God places images inside every new creation, but lots of junk (ignorance, misinformation, bad experiences, etc.) bury these truths. As ministers, it's our job to chisel away the junk to expose God's realities. Like Michelangelo—he said he'd look at a piece of marble and think, "I see an angel in it." Then he would chisel away the stone around the angel to "set it free." And what was left was beautiful!

LOOK BEYOND WHAT YOUR EYES SEE

The Bible says God wishes that all men would be saved, but He doesn't stop there. He also desires that we would come to the complete and full knowledge of Him (1 Timothy 2:4), which I see you accomplishing. Jesus was able to look beyond natural circumstances and create images in people's hearts. Remember when He went into a household where a little girl died? Everyone was crying. Jesus looked at the little girl and said, "She's not

dead, she's just sleeping." Jesus was not lying. He knew a greater reality. A greater reality than even death had come—Jesus the
life-giver. He told them she wasn't dead to change their image
in their hearts. They laughed, but Jesus moved them out of the
room and raised the little girl from the dead. In His heart, He saw
beyond what "was."

God calls the things that be not as though they were (Romans 4:17). God sees us as complete in Him, even though we see
our incompleteness. God sees us in His fullness and holiness,
and as we see things as He does, they will become fact.

SEEING OTHERS AS JESUS DOES

Have you ever had trouble with a Christian brother or sis-
ter? Well, I have. One time in particular, I went to God in prayer
because a certain Christian brother just didn't like me. He was
in an important position to give teachers and preachers opportunities to minister, but he wouldn't let me—even though he knew
I was quite ready and capable. I was so angry! So I told God
on him. I told God how awful this brother was, and how much
he needed to be changed or removed. But God spoke and said,
"Claudia—I can't hear you." So I spoke louder!

But it was not my volume that prevented God from hearing
me. It was my accusations. God told me that the man I prayed
about was his servant, and that He didn't see him the same way

as I did. But He said that if I would begin to see him like God did, my prayers would be heard. If I'd call the things that be not as though they were, better things would happen. God said, "As you think in your heart concerning him, you will see it happen."

So I began to change my image of this man. I saw him full of the fruits of the Holy Spirit, full of love, joy, peace, patience, kindness and self-control. I saw him walking as Jesus did, in love and kindness. I not only got a new image of him, I also saw in the Word that I had favor with God and man. I then began expecting this man to ask me to teach, even bending over backwards to let me minister. As I changed my picture, God said, "Now you have presented a correct picture before me. That picture will act as faith unto me and it shall be done according to your faith." Within a few weeks, I saw a dramatic change in this man's behavior. Where there was once dominance, now there was kindness. I saw his dislike for me become favor toward me! It's a principle—as we think of others, so they will be.

WE'RE NOT WHO WE USED TO BE

It is natural for human beings to be around people who like them. No one enjoys being with people who hate them. We like to be around people who like us, admire us, and think highly of us, because deep down inside of us, that's the true image God, has given us of ourselves. God doesn't want us to be ashamed. He doesn't want us to feel like we are below the standard of Christ's own perfection. He loved us so much that He sent Jesus to come and die for us. We have been given the righteous nature of Jesus Christ, and that makes us worthy enough. That's the reason we must develop the correct image of ourselves and others.

When we were born again, the Bible says we became a new creation, a brand-new person; that old things passed away, and that the fresh and the new has come (See 2 Corinthians 5:17). In 2 Corinthians 5:15-16 it states, *"And that he died for all, that they which live should not henceforth live unto themselves, but unto him which died for them, and rose again. Wherefore henceforth know we no man after the flesh: yea, though we have known Christ after the flesh, yet now henceforth know we him no more."*

When Jesus walked the earth, He was looked upon by many as simply an ordinary man. He was regarded from merely a human standpoint. But He was more than a human being—he was a spirit being, one with God the Father. The Word says that we are wrong when we view Him only from a human standpoint.

Furthermore, we should no longer recognize anyone who is in Christ from a merely human point of view. We cannot regard our brothers and sisters from a natural rather than a spiritual perspective. They, along with us, are one with the Father, one with Christ, and one with the Spirit. When He became sin, we were set free from sin (2 Corinthians 5:21). When He died, we died (2

Corinthians 5:14). We were resurrected with Him and are seated with Him (Ephesians 2:6).

Therefore, we no longer can regard ourselves from a human standpoint any more than we can regard Jesus from a human standpoint. We are spirit beings. As we awake to our righteousness in Him, we will not sin (1 Corinthians 15:34). As we walk in His fullness, we'll no longer be empty. As we walk in His righteousness, we'll no longer walk in selfishness.

Jesus wants that picture permanently etched on the inside of us. As we get this picture inside us, we will walk in it. When God gave me this message, I saw it help a lot of people see circumstances change. When we see an area in a brother's life that isn't right, we'll not judge him, but we'll speak the truth according to the Word. We'll receive and transmit the right picture! If he is angry, we'll see him peaceful; and the words of our mouths will line up with that picture. We will not be lying—we're telling the truth, just as Jesus wasn't lying when He said, "the child's not dead, but sleeping."

We have the same authority. Get the right picture of yourself and your friends, your children, your parents, or your husband or wife. Speak good words over them—even if outwardly it seems untrue. Your words will create pictures on the inside of them. When I preach on healing, I create pictures on the inside of the sick being healed. Words create a picture, and when the picture is there, it acts as faith to God. Then healing comes! When I preach on the Holy Spirit, the words create pictures—they build faith—and people are filled with the Holy Spirit.

CHANGING THE NEGATIVES

So often, I go to churches that talk about how lazy Christians are, that we're not doing our job, that we must clean ourselves up, so we can be a "spotless bride" presented to Christ. But the Bible says He has perfected us and that we have been (past tense) cleansed and are now a spotless bride (Ephesians 5:27). In Hebrews 10:14, we read: *"For by one offering he hath perfected for ever them that are sanctified."* By a single offering it was forever done!

Unfortunately, the picture in many hearts is that of a struggling Christian, not a victorious one. Sometimes we see ourselves as unrighteous sinners, but God says we're righteous. We may see ourselves sick, and yet God says we are healed by His stripes (Isaiah 53:5). We then pray in unbelief: "God please heal me." But He has. *"Who his own self bare our sins in his own body on the tree; that we, being dead to sins, should live unto righteousness: by whose stripes ye were healed,"* —1 Peter 2:24. Not by his wounds you may be healed, or even will be healed. But by His wounds you are healed. Get the image inside you!

Don't concentrate on sickness when healing will overcome it. It's like being hungry in a room with a feast set before you.

Why concentrate on the hunger when the food will satisfy it? Why concentrate on sickness when healing has come? Why concentrate on sin when righteousness has come?

We need to get this picture—for every problem that arises, there is an answer in Christ. The reason we meditate on the Word day and night is so it will paint the correct images on the canvas of our heart. The negative picture the devil would place there is, "Look out for number one." But the Word says, *"Think of others before yourself,"* (Romans 12:10), and *"Lay your life down and lose your life,"* (John 15:12-13).

The negative says, "Keep all your money so you can be taken care of." But the Bible says, *"Give and it shall be given to you,"* Luke 6:38. *"Cast thy bread upon the waters: for thou shalt find it after many days,"* Ecclesiastes 11:1. Romans 6:22 says, *"But now being made free from sin, and become servants to God, ye have your fruit unto holiness, and the end everlasting life."* "But now! But now!"

We've been set free from sin. So why are we trying so hard to get victory in areas where we already have it? We have already overcome the evil one (1 John 4:4). Jesus has already defeated the devil for us. He made a bold display of the devil while He was on the cross (Colossians 2:15).

When Jesus was on the cross, His life looked like total failure. The disciples thought He would be the next King of Israel, but there was; their King Jesus, on the cross, bleeding and dying. But something was happening that their physical eyes could not see—Jesus was taking away our sin. Mankind's sickness was upon Him. Jesus was becoming one with our old nature, one with our sin. Then He died in that nature, went to hell, and stripped Satan of all his power. Satan no longer would be our father, because Jesus revealed God the Father. Jesus had stripped Satan of all authority to lay hold of any part of us.

Get this picture inside you—Jesus bound-up and paraded the principalities and powers of hell before the host of Heaven. In ancient times, when warriors won a battle, they would parade the defeated kings and rulers before the conquering nation. Jesus did the same with Satan. Satan was forever stripped, bound and humiliated before all!

Sometimes when I'm in prayer, and I have an area in my life I'm being tempted in, I parade that area, bound and subject to the Word, before all of heaven. I see it chained up and defeated. Jesus is my victor! I get that picture in me. When Jesus paraded Satan, I'm sure the heavenly host laughed and rejoiced. So should we.

GOD'S PICTURE OF US

In Luke 1:37, it says, *"With God, nothing is impossible."* No Word from God shall go without fulfillment. God's Word is truth, no matter what you see or feel. There was a time when I did not see myself as a minister. I desired to be a minister, but I didn't think I really would ever be one. But I changed the picture in my heart. I saw myself preaching everywhere, even in foreign countries, because God told me to do it in His Word. He commanded me to go into all the world and preach (Matthew 28:19). Long before I ever preached in other countries, I saw it in my heart. Then it came to pass. I saw us writing books and producing tapes. I saw us ministering to the lost, preaching words of encouragement to the church. And now it's happening! God's Word is truth, so I continue to put it on the inside of me.

"Being born again, not of corruptible seed, but of incorruptible, by the word of God, which liveth and abideth for ever," —1 Peter 1:23. The Word is God's sperm, His essence. His Word impregnates us. We are continually giving birth to the things of God.

Read 1 John 3:9: *"Whosoever is born of God doth not commit sin; for his seed remaineth in him: and he cannot sin, because he is born of God."* We've been trying to get victory over sinning. Yet the Bible says if we are born of God, we can't practice sin. We may sin accidentally, but as born again Christians we can't practice sinning. We practice to get good at using God's Word. Jesus became as we are, and His victory over Satan was our victory. Jesus overcame Satan for us, taking our punishment and giving us His righteousness. We need to understand the picture of the old man and his nature as being dead. The new man is alive! It is no longer us that lives, but Christ. We will then walk in the full victory that

Christ purchased for us.

WE ARE LIKE OUR FATHER

I have pictures in my heart that I've not yet seen the manifestation of—but I will!   The pictures I have in my heart are according to God's Word, and they will be fulfilled. I have grasped that "... *as a man thinketh, so is he*" (Proverbs 23:7). Before I minister, I come before the Father and ask Him to give me a picture of what will happen. I see faces; I see the response of people to the message. Jesus said, "I only do that which I've seen the Father do." So I pray to see what the Father will be doing in the service. Then, when I minister, I've already seen it—so I act it out. Some ministers say, "This is going to be a hard message, and most of you won't receive it." Well, they've put the negative picture forth, and it will come to pass. I'd prefer to say, "Everyone will receive this message, and it will change your life!"

We are not our own. Therefore, we have no right to have a poverty mentality, or any other negative pictures of ourselves or others. I put a new picture in my heart—instead of needing money, I see myself giving to others. I took the image of fear and replaced it with abundance. You, too, must replace the negatives with the image that God creates in His Word. It doesn't matter whether you feel it or not—just receive it at His Word. It doesn't matter if you feel perfected and completed. The Word says it, so see it and receive it!

Why have negatives? They produce negative faith. Why not have faith, the substance? Faith, the picture? Then, you'll produce Godly fruit. Give God a complete picture of what He says we are—a reflection of Him! Why not get into agreement with God about what He says we are? As we do, we paint accurate pictures that act as faith. Without faith, it's impossible to please God (Hebrews 11:6). With faith, we delight Him. The Bible says "...*as He is, so are we in this world,*" (1 John 4:17). Is God sick? Depressed? Confused? No! He's full of life, joy and love. So, too, are we!

The fullness of the Godhead dwells inside us. We have no less ability than Christ did when He walked the earth. For us to live is Christ (Philippians 1:21), and we have the same authority as Jesus did. We have the same right to approach the Father as Jesus did! We are the branches; He is the Vine (John 15:5). We are one (John 17:21). He is the Head; we are the body (Ephesians 5:23). That's the image Jesus wants in our hearts—not a negative sign, not an ugly picture, but a correct picture of us and of others. See Jesus in yourself. See Him in others. We can partake of our answer—the image of God in us.

So I ask you: if I gave you a piece of paper and told you to draw a picture of anyone you would want to become, or what kind of life you'd like to be living—who or what would you draw? Go ahead and do it. Use God's Word as your blueprint. Because as a man thinks in his heart, so is he! ❈

PART VI

HOW TO BEAR UP UNDER SUFFERING

"I have learned,
in whatsoever state I am, therewith **to be content."**
Philippians 4:11

HOW TO BEAR UP UNDER SUFFERING

Many people don't want to hear or study about suffering. They say, "I have enough suffering without studying about it." I thought the same way! But God showed me how suffering can bring real victory in our lives. A friend said to me, "I just don't understand why people must suffer so much. They get so far under, that when they look up they just see pebbles." As she spoke, I imagined looking up and just seeing a pebble.

Then I heard a conversation inside me, the Holy Spirit talking to Jesus. He said, "If my people knew what suffering was, they would be having altar calls for suffering. If they only understood the victory of suffering." I spoke these same words to my friend, and we both knew the Holy Spirit had spoken a truth that we must try to understand. I began my study on suffering, and I am telling you that the wisdom I've acquired has held me through traumatic events. I have remained strong in

Him because of what He has shown me.

When I think of suffering, I remember as a child going to the hospital and seeing my aunt. She was dying, and everyone said, "She's suffering so much." The term "suffering" that we use in our natural mind means someone is moaning and groaning in pain and agony. We think that is how a person suffers.

But there is a Bible definition of suffering. It means to bear up under. Not to ache and hurt, but to bear up under. There have been many situations I've come through, thinking that I was suffering—but it was not the Bible kind of suffering. I didn't bear up under the situation. Quite the opposite—I was put under by the circumstances.

We need to be like Shadrach, Meshach and Abednego— the three men in the fiery furnace. When they went through the fire, not even the smell of smoke was on them. When you go through the fire, you shall not be burned. When you go across the river, it shall not overtake you. You shall not drown. That's how to suffer like Christ suffered.

Think of this: I'm in a dark alley, and someone comes up to attack me. But I am walking with a 6'9" tall, 300 pound, mean-looking body-builder. Wouldn't it be ridiculous for me to fight the attacker? I wouldn't need to fight that person because I have my powerful friend with me. So many times we don't understand that we have Christ Jesus inside us. But so often when trials come, we think we have to go through it by ourselves.

Remember—the real definition of suffering is "to bear up under." If I tried to pick up a piano, the weight of it would crush me. But if I had four strong men to help me lift it, it would be no problem. That's what God wants us to know about suffering. It's no problem, because He is with us! Remember what Jesus said to His disciples in John 16:7? He said, *"I'm going away, but I send the Holy Spirit to remain with you. You'll not be left as orphans."* Here is Matthew's account in Matthew 28:19-20, *"Go into all the world and preach"* and *"Lo, I am with you always. I am the one who is with you wherever you go."*

It would be like me saying to you, "Go to the store and buy groceries." If I told you to go to the store and buy groceries, it would be because I intended to give you the money to buy them. Jesus says, "Go into all the world and preach." Why? Because He's providing us with everything we need to go to all the world and preach. He is inside us.

Here is the struggle—we see a situation coming up, and we are devastated by the potential outcome. Maybe the circumstance is a lost job or a lost relationship. But the Bible tells us how to overcome circumstances. Paul says, "I've learned the secret of living."

So what is the secret of living?

Philippians 4:11-13 provides us with some excellent advice on that question, *"Not that I speak in respect of want: for I have learned, in whatsoever state I am, therewith to be content. I know both how to be abased, and I know how to abound: everywhere and in all things I am instructed both to be full and to be hungry, both to abound and to suffer need. I can do all things through Christ which strengtheneth me."*

This is the secret of living—to be independent of circumstances. I am going to give you many scriptures in this book so this "secret" can go deep inside you. Many people reading this book right now are going through adverse circumstances. If you're not, don't worry—they'll come soon enough!

WHEN TRIALS COME, REJOICE!

I have finally learned to obey the Bible. It says when trials come, rejoice! (James 1:2). I used to read that and think, "Come on—when trials come, rejoice? When trials come, I'm supposed to laugh? Right!" The preacher asks, "Who has a testimony today?" We raise our hands and say, "Yes, oh, joy, I'm in a trial, it's the worst it's ever been!" No—that's not the kind of joy the Bible speaks of. The joy the Bible speaks of is a state of being, not an emotion that changes with the circumstances. The terms "joy" and "strength" are interchangeable in the Bible. We can go through a trial with the strength of God. The joy of the Lord is our strength; or, the strength of the Lord is our joy. He will put us over the trial with His strength. So we can be joyful!

Still, I am convinced that we haven't hooked-in to the joy of going through a trial because we still see trials and suffering as something very bad coming against us. But Jesus doesn't view it like that, and the Bible doesn't see it that way. Let's look at the Bible's perspective in Hebrews 2:10: *"For it became him, for whom are all things, and by whom are all things, in bringing many sons unto glory, to make the captain of their salvation perfect through sufferings."*

It was an act worthy of God and fitting to the divine that Jesus should go through suffering so He could be a perfect High Priest. Many times we think, "I don't want to go through these things that are happening!" But we are no greater than our Master (John 13:16), and if our Master and Teacher had to go through suffering to learn perfection, then who are we to say, "I won't do it"?

I remember a minister saying he had a staff member who stole money from his offerings. The minister went before God and said, "How could you have allowed this to happen?" Jesus spoke and told him, "You're no greater than your Master. I had a thief in My ministry, and now so do you!" We will go through things just as our Master did. In Hebrews 2:17-18 it says, *"Wherefore in all things it behooved him to be made like unto his brethren, that he might be a merciful and faithful high priest in things pertaining to God, to make reconciliation for the sins of the people. For in that he himself hath suffered being tempted, he is able to succour them that are tempted."*

OUR ARK OF SAFETY

Jesus is able to run to our cry—but not so He can pull us out of the trial so that we won't have to suffer. The Word says He comes to our aid because we are going through the sufferings He went through. He understands, and He has well-timed help coming just when we need it!

I wish there was another way, too—I really do. I wish there was another method that the Father had for us to grow. I wish we could come to a perfect place in life and never have another problem. But that's not how we grow, and that's not the divine plan. God doesn't do anything or give anything harmful to us, does He?

Have you ever tried to feed a baby vegetables? They want only the sweet stuff. They don't want what is good for them—the things that will make them grow. Or, when an athlete is in training, there are things he does that are painful, but that prepares him for the upcoming event. If you're training for a tournament in karate, you must learn how to block blows as well as take them. I remember training for karate tournaments when I was a teenager, and having to do 300 sit-ups a day. We would push and push ourselves until we were so tired I thought we would die!

But when the contest came, we were ready. There are things we are going through right now that are preparing us for the spiritual battles of the end times.

I want to make this clear—God does not bring trials to us. It's the devil that does that. Besides, it's not the trials that come to us that equip us; it's how and what we do with these trials that equips us—or that crushes us. In Revelation 3:10, there's a Scripture that is often misquoted. People incorrectly read it to say, "God will keep you from the hour of trial." But what the Word actually says is, *"God will keep you safe from the hour of trial."*

You can look at Noah. The flood was coming, and it came on Noah just like everyone else. But Noah was inside the ark. And the water—the same water that drowned other people—lifted Noah and the ark up. It's the same thing with trials. Either trials will overtake us and drown us, or we'll use them to lift us up to a higher spiritual place. When we go through them with Christ as our ark of safety, they will be that which lifts us up! Look in 1 Peter 4:1-2: *"Forasmuch then as Christ hath suffered for us in the flesh, arm yourselves likewise with the same mind: for he that hath suffered in the flesh hath ceased from sin, that he no longer should live the rest of his time in the flesh for the lusts of men, but for the will of God."*

We need to have the same mind as Christ Jesus did. We need to be ready to suffer—to bear up under—as Christ Jesus did. Think of the sufferings of Christ. We see Christ's sufferings as agonizing times. But doesn't it just blow your mind to think

that He endured the cross for the joy that was set before Him
(Hebrews 12:2)?

The word "endure" is the same Greek root word as "suffering" and "patience." *"But let patience have her perfect work,
that ye may be perfect and entire, wanting nothing,"* James 1:4. Let
suffering and endurance have their perfect work, so you'll be
perfect and entire. Let's grasp hold of what the scripture says:
When we go through suffering as Christ, we do away with
intentional sin. Having a sin problem? Go through it with
Christ Jesus.

Jesus stood before Pilate, who mockingly asked, "Who are
You? They say You're the King of the Jews." Put yourself in Jesus' place so you can understand endurance and suffering. He is
the God who created the heavens and earth; it was He who made
man out of the dirt. And dirt was looking at God and asking,
"Who do You say that You are?" Realize the level of suffering
and endurance He experienced right then. The temptation must
have been great to prove Himself as Almighty God rather than to
make Himself a sacrifice for mankind at the cross.

But He didn't yield to emotion—he held fast to His confession by saying, "I am a King," John 18:37. At the cross, He
suffered for the joy that was set before him (Hebrews 12:2). He
endured the cross for you and me—we were the joy that was
set before Him. We see the Hollywood portrayal of Jesus going

to the cross in total sorrow. But He was full of joy, because He knew the final outcome. And in bad situations, the only way to have victory is to be like Paul—independent of circumstances. Jesus saw past His circumstances, saw past the cross, and saw you and me.

Look at 1 Peter 3:18, *"For Christ also hath once suffered for sins, the just for the unjust, that he might bring us to God, being put to death in the flesh, but quickened by the Spirit."* Christ, the Just made unjust, the Righteous Man made unrighteous.

Consider Paul, the Apostle—Jesus appeared to him. He appeared to him and taught him! Paul probably envisioned that he would have the largest, most successful and prosperous ministry of anyone. So what happens to him? He gets thrown in jail. Now, that's suffering and endurance time! Paul had his choice—to do it the Bible way, or the natural way. While in jail, he could have cried, "I can't believe it—God told me about my ministry, and it's not working! Why? Is it my prayer life? Lack of faith? Or is it sin in my life? Is someone praying against me, cursing me?"

He could have tormented himself. He could have blamed God. He could have blamed Silas. But Silas and Paul prayed and sang to God, and the jail was opened! Because Paul handled his trial the Bible way, going through it instead of being cursed by it, his ministry continues today. How many ministers can you say that about? Two thousand years later, Paul still is vital in the ministry.

THE BIGGEST FEAR

The biggest fear man has is dying. Someone will break into your house. End result—they'll kill you. Someone will steal all your money, and then you'll be broke and live on the street and die. Death—that's the biggest fear! But God has taken that fear from Christians by giving us eternal life. The worst thing that could ever happen is to die, but for us it's the best thing! There is no fear in death. Christ defused it. If the fear is that someone will take away all our stuff— so what? They can never take Jesus, so there is no fear in anything!

The Bible says 365 times, "fear not." That's one "fear not" for every day of the year. In James 5:10, 11, & 13 it says: "Take, my brethren, the prophets, who have spoken in the name of the Lord, for an example of suffering affliction, and of patience. Behold, we count them happy which endure. Ye have heard of the patience of Job, and have seen the end of the Lord; that the Lord is very pitiful, and of tender mercy."

This key Scripture talks of the prophets of old, and how they suffered and endured as it was God's plan to add unto them blessings. It says when you suffer and you are confronted with trials you should pray, because there's only One who can help you. But most commonly, when we find ourselves in a trial, we go from person to person asking them to pray for us: "Will you pray for me? You can't imagine what I'm going through." But the Bible says in verses 13-15 of James 5, *"Is any among you afflicted? Let him pray. Is any merry? Let him sing psalms. Is any sick among you? Let him call for the elders of the church; and let them pray over him, anointing him with oil in the name of the Lord: And the prayer of faith shall save the sick, and the Lord shall raise him up. . ."*

Think about it—I would venture to say that almost every time sickness has really come strong in your natural body, you had been oppressed of the devil just a short time before. That's why it says, "When oppressed of the devil, pray." You must pray. If you don't pray, there's still another way out—call the elders and you'll be healed. But you'll have to go around the mountain again. I'll tell you the truth, we've been around and around the mountain in our ministry so many times that when adversity comes, instead of quitting, getting angry or frustrated—we know we can go through it! We can go through with Jesus.

First-time travelers on ministry trips with us have such a hard time. When the devil throws his usual defeating darts, they begin to cry and say, "This must not be God. It's so hard." But we know it must be God, not by the comfort or difficulty of a situation, but by the Spirit. Circumstances don't dictate God's will for us!

Once I was "suffering"—and I thought it would never end. But God spoke to me and said, "Claudia, never mistake a temporary situation for a state-of-being." I'll say it again so you can receive it for yourself—never mistake a temporary situation for a state-of-being. Right now, you may be in a temporary bad situation or temporary trial, but that is not your state-of-being. Make this confession: "My state-of-being is righteousness, joy, and love. My state-of-being is oneness with Christ Jesus in all of His fullness." That's my state-of-being. That's eternity.

OUR STATE OF BEING

Don't mistake a temporary situation for a state-of-being in your life just because it's so intense. We have a tendency to live in only the circumstance of the moment, feeling it will never end. But it's temporary! We need to be caught up in our state-of-being, not the situation. I've learned that when situations opposing me come, they will pass.

I like the song that says, "Don't worry, be happy." And I say, "Don't worry, be happy, it's going to be better because Jesus is still on the throne!" It sounds too simple, but it's the truth. I've seen man rise and fall, but Jesus is forever seated on the throne. It helps me to remember that I am in Christ Jesus. The Bible tells us we are joint heirs with Him. The Way Bible[1] translation says,

1 Arthur S. Way, *Letters of Paul, Hebrews and the Book of Psalms.*
(Grand Rapids, Kegel Publications, 1981).

"We share His throne." That is so incredible! We have the right to His throne—His dominion—because He gave it to us. We also have the right to share His sufferings. But remember—He goes through it with us. We saw in 1 Peter that when we go through suffering, we do away with intentional sin. We don't please ourselves, but we please God. I want to be pleasing to God. When trials come, I want to be so pleasing to God that I say to Him, "Let's go through it together." I want to rejoice in suffering.

SATAN'S MONKEY WRENCH

One time we were getting ready for a ministry tour in Mexico. We had just bought our bus. We used every dime we had and had taken out a large loan as well, to pay for it. A man had volunteered to remodel it for us before our trip, which was then two-and-a-half months away. After two months, we found he had not done any work on the bus. We were so discouraged! All our finances, our hopes, and our dreams were invested in this bus.

So we decided to encourage ourselves by putting the couch in the bus. At least then we could see a little of the vision complete. Five hours later, we were still trying to cram the couch in the bus door! I had fallen in love with the couches at the store, but I didn't measure them to see if they'd fit in the bus door. We had to use five people and a crow bar to force it into the bus.

Once we got it in the bus, I realized it was on the wrong side of the bus—it had to be turned around! So we had to take it out and put it right. Once the couch was in there, we encouraged ourselves by packing our clothes and food in this empty bus (empty except for the sofa!).

"God's called us and we're going!" we said. We decided to drive by a friend's office to "show off" the bus on the way out of town to Mexico. As we got to his office, the bus stalled right there. It wouldn't start for hours, but we finally got it to the seller's shop. The shop told us they'd get it fixed in 12 hours. We waited, and in 12 hours we were on the road to Mexico again. About 15 miles out of town, the bus started smoking inside. Our new (to us) bus was filled with smoke—then we heard a noise like pots and pans clanging in the engine. We had blown the engine. After driving 15 miles—on our very first trip in the bus—our engine blew! So we cried out, "God! You've called us—you told us to get this bus—what do we do now?"

We were still able to drive back to the shop where they told us the engine was totally blown. We decided that we were not going anywhere—we were not calling anyone. God would have to help us if He wanted us in Mexico. He could move us if He wanted to, but we weren't going anywhere without His assistance. We lived in the back lot of the bus company. I'd open up a can of soup and fixed it in the microwave. We slept on the floor, but we would not move. We acted like we were on our trip.

At the same time we were at the back lot, friends were praying for us. God spoke to them and said, "Take your van, fuel it up, and go to the bus company, so I can bless you." They thought that God would bless them with a bus! Meanwhile in the bus we prayed, "God, we know You're faithful and will send us to Mexico."

Soon the people who were praying for us came to the bus shop. They told the owner, "We're here with our van, and we'd like to see the buses for sale like Claudia and Wyatt bought."

The owner said, "Oh, Claudia and Wyatt? They're in our back lot."

The people who brought the truck said, "No, they're in Mexico. We saw them off three days ago!"

"No, they're in the back!" They came to the bus and knocked on our door. I was eating soup and reading. Remember, nobody knew we were in town. After explaining our situation, they realized why God had them fuel their van—so they could lend it to us to go to Mexico. Within two hours, we were on our way. Glory to God! The meetings in Mexico were incredible. In this situation, we suffered with Christ. We didn't let the problems crush us. We bore up under adverse circumstances. Nowadays, if the bus breaks down we know God will always take care of it. So we don't worry—we keep our joy.

First-time travelers with us, who haven't been through

the fire and have not been refined, almost go crazy because of all the things that happen and go wrong. To us who have been through it before, it's no big deal. I saw a vision of Satan throwing in a monkey wrench to keep the first man from finishing our bus. The devil wanted to discourage us and keep us from going on the trip. But he looks up—and we're still going. Then Satan says, "Well, I'll keep the couch from going in there. That will stop them!" He looks again, and we finally get it in with the crow bar. We're still going. Then he says, "Their engine will blow up—that will stop them!" But it didn't, much to his dismay. We think of Satan as spoiling our plans, but as Christians, we're spoiling his plans daily. He's not effective coming against our plans—we're effective coming against his!

SHARE SUFFERING WITH CHRIST

Much of the reason we don't experience the glory (the manifested presence of God) in our lives is because we run from suffering. If we will go through suffering, His glory will be revealed. *"And if children, then heirs; heirs of God, and joint-heirs with Christ; if so be that we suffer with him, that we may be also glorified together; For I reckon that the sufferings of this present time are not worthy to be compared with the glory which shall be revealed in us,"* —Romans 8:17-18.

That's what the sufferings do—they bring glory in us, on

us, through us. But we must share sufferings with Christ. The key word is with Christ. Suffering alone does no good. But when we are with Christ, in Him, that's when we come out without the smell of smoke. That's where the victory is, that's where the glory is. Suffering is used to bring us our inheritance. Then the glory will come through us, and on to others. It's the manifested presence of God working through you and me.

Do you know why the presence of God is so evident in some people? Because they have gone through it. When you're in a situation where you can't do anything on your own, remember—you can do all things through Christ (Philippians 4:13). It's Him inside us that strengthens us. If there was a way to put a musician inside me, I could play an instrument or do anything he could do. But it's Christ inside me, and I can do all the things that He does. If He goes through suffering with joy, so can I.

In Hebrews chapters 11, 12, and 13, many great heroes of faith are mentioned. Notice that there was a key in their lives that made them great. Look at Noah—while building the ark, everyone made fun of him because no one had seen catastrophic rain before. But he knew and had a vision of the things to come. Abraham, in the midst of mockers, said he'd be a father. He had a vision of a city whose builder and architect was God (Hebrews 11:10). They were able to do great works because they had a vision—not of here and now in their bad circumstances, but of the future and a heavenly vision.

VISIONS OF ETERNITY

We must have a deeper appreciation of eternal life. If we could only grasp hold of eternity, we would live so differently! I believe we wouldn't worry about silly problems. We'd be looking to get people into the kingdom! I ask God to put the reality of eternity in us right now. The men of faith had visions of eternity, which enabled them to do things here on earth—so can we. Look in your Bible at 2 Corinthians 4:17-18: "For our light affliction, which is but for a moment, worketh for us a far more exceeding and eternal weight of glory; While we look not at the things which are seen: but at the things which are not seen: for the things which are seen are temporal; but the things which are not seen are eternal.

It says these momentary afflictions will produce His glory in you if you'll go through them. It's a glory that will never cease. We'll not look at problems here and now, but we'll look past the problems to the answer. We look to the things that be not as though they were. We don't just see the problems—we see the victory! That's God's realm. I'm talking about not worrying. Not having to go through the pain—the natural pain.

I'll suffer with Christ, I'm going to endure and brace up with Christ. I'm going through this water with a life jacket on. I am not staying in it; I'm going through with Christ. Remember, suffering is not to break down under circumstances. It's not, "poor me." Suffering is to bear up under and pass through.

THE POWER OF LOVE

With love, we bear up under anything and everything that comes. Love is inside you. Think about that—Love suffers long. Love long endures, and is patient and kind (says 1 Corinthians 13:4). When one member of the body suffers, the whole body suffers (1 Corinthians 12:26). Think about that, using the Bible definition of suffering. When one member of the body bears up, the whole body bears up. When I go through fire, not only my legs go through it, but my whole body goes through it too. We are not our own. I can't say, "Oh, I don't know whether I am going to bear up in this trial. I'm real tired. I can't do that."

I'm not mine. I have a responsibility to God—and to you, because you're part of me. If I don't bear up under, neither do you. And if you don't bear up under and come through, neither do I.

We owe it by obligation to walk as He walked (1 John 2:26). We owe it to God; I owe it to you to love you. That means walking in His victory so you can too! That means I owe everything. Owe love? That's expensive. I wish God would have said, "Owe no man nothing more than ten dollars." I'd pay you off and be through with it! But I owe it to you to love you. Love is patient and kind. It endures everything. That's what love is. So when you're going through something, realize it's not just for yourself. You'll be purified for the benefit of the rest of the body. We will all reap the results of that which you've gone through!

THE FIERY TRIAL

First Peter 4:12-14 explains, *"Beloved, think it not strange concerning the fiery trial which is to try you, as though some strange thing happened unto you: But rejoice, inasmuch as ye are partakers of Christ's sufferings; that, when his glory shall be revealed, ye may be glad also with exceeding joy. If ye be reproached for the name of Christ, happy are ye; for the spirit of glory and of God resteth upon you: on their part he is evil spoken of, but on your part he is glorified."*

Isn't that phenomenal? The Spirit of Glory is upon us. God says to not be surprised or amazed when trials come, but sometimes I still get surprised and amazed. Sometimes I don't know why things are happening. But God says not to be amazed when ordeals come to test your quality. Because I'm in Christ, when trials come to test my quality, it tests His quality. His quality always comes out as pure gold.

When Satan came to tempt Jesus, he came with a season—a cycle—of temptation (Luke 4:13). There are cycles of temptation that will come to you. After Satan's cycle of temptation ended, the Bible says he left to wait for a more opportune time. Know that when Satan leaves, he will always wait for a more opportune time to return. But that's no reason to fear. After all, because of your resistance to his temptations, he had to leave you. If he was so powerful, why did he have to leave? The Christ in you, the Word inside you, has made you as pure gold. The Spirit of Glory rests upon you and is inside you. Read 1 Peter 5:10, "*But the God of all grace, who hath called us unto his eternal glory by Christ Jesus, after that ye have suffered a while, make you perfect, establish, strengthen, settle you.*"

God Himself will make you what you ought to be when you go through the sufferings of Christ. The Bible tells us to do the works of Him who sent us. You know what's inseparable from your vocation? Suffering is inseparable from your vocation, bearing up under circumstances. It's part of the job, but it's also our privilege, the privilege of sharing His suffering. We obviously have had the wrong definition of suffering. If not, why would God call it a privilege? But God understands the blessings of suffering. He understands it's the way to perfect us. We've been through many trials, and we're better people, aren't we? Don't you wish it wasn't true? But it is!

You're a different person because you bore up under trials. However, many others haven't—they've been crushed. But there's a way to go through trials more successfully than you've been able to before—go through them in the same way Christ did. The Bible tells us to set our minds to endure suffering in the same way He did, to have the vision of eternity; to have the vision of victory.

If you're in a trial, go through it with Jesus so your quality can be tested. God has counted you and me worthy to go through trials and temptations. He promises that we're not tempted beyond our ability to endure. These great trials should show you that you have a great ability to endure. It's not too hard—it's not—because we are not alone. We have Christ Jesus.

GOD'S FAITHFULNESS

When Jesus walked on the earth, the Holy Spirit did the works through Him. The fullness of the Godhead dwelled in Him and dwells in us. Jesus wasn't alone, and neither are we. He didn't leave us orphans. But He did send One to comfort us, to strengthen us, to stand by us, to be our advocate, to be with us at all times—He sent the Holy Spirit to us. You're not going through things that no one else has gone through, and you're not feeling things that no one else has ever felt. Stop thinking that way—feel Jesus and His victory. Then, when trials come, we will look for the victory. When our car stops running, we look for the glory. Watch God manifest Himself! When the bill collectors are at the door, rejoice and watch God's completion at work in you. He says, *"I will never, no never, leave or forsake you,"* —Hebrews 13:5. This means He will not leave you without financial support. Watch God's faithfulness—when it looks like I can't hang on any longer, I remember that in my weakness, He is made strong. He can always hang on. Glory to God!

We've begun to see trials differently. We rejoice that we are counted worthy. Remember, there is nothing that can stop you. The devil will try to bring discouragement. But if you will keep your eyes on Jesus, discouragement will not be able to hold you back. You win every time! If discouragement gets you, you begin to lose. So shake it off and go through the circumstances. Stay in Christ and let His joy be your strength! Remember, joy and strength have the same root word. You can interchange the words "joy" and "strength" in your Bible. Jesus is full of joy and full of strength. He's in me, so I'm full of joy and strength. Be independent of your circumstances—master the secret of living. It was God's will for Jesus to go through suffering, and it's His will for us to go through and bear up under adverse circumstances. Just keep your eyes on Jesus Christ, the author of your faith. ❁

PART VII

THEREFORE CELEBRATE!

"And the people were full of a sense of celebration—
all that giving! And all given willingly, freely!
King David was exuberant."
1 Chronicles 29:9, The Message

THEREFORE, CELEBRATE!

I love the Word of God. It can pull me out of any circumstance, out of any situation, out of anything that seems so limiting to me—the Word of God. And it is such an honor to be able to have the Word of God and to be able to take it personally. God really has fulfilled us, and His fullness is really—really, on the inside of us. It's all about Him, and what He's created us to be—in Him—is incredible.

As we read these scriptures, I want you to take Him personally. I want you to receive the Word the way it's supposed to be received—as though God was speaking it directly to you. Because I'm telling you that God is speaking to you and His Word is alive and full of power.

THE FULLNESS OF THE GODHEAD

"For in him dwelleth all the fullness of the Godhead bodily. And ye are complete in him, which is the head of all principality and power: In whom also ye are circumcised with the circumcision made without hands, in putting off the body of the sins of the flesh by the circumcision of Christ," —Colossians 2:9-11.

Now I want you to pay close attention, that there was a circumcision done, but not a natural circumcision. And I'll tell you: even a natural circumcision—you wouldn't want it done every day, I would imagine. It's done once. But yet we come up with doctrines that say, "we must die daily." There is something that we have to do every day—receive what God has already done.

The Word says, "He stripped off the old." And it says, "The fullness of the Godhead dwelled in Jesus." Now I want you to imagine what that is—the fullness of the Father, the fullness of the Holy Spirit, dwelt in bodily form in Jesus. Everything that Jesus did was not from some gifting, some partial thing of God—it was the fullness of the Father, the fullness of the Son. And in Him we now have the fullness of the Father, the fullness of the Son and the fullness of the Spirit, dwelling in bodily form.

Now when it says, "He had the fullness of the Godhead dwelling in Him," it meant to give complete expression of the divine nature. You and I also have the fullness of God dwelling in us so we can have the full expression of Who God is—He is the Master, He is the Almighty, He is the Healer, He is the Redeemer. All that He is, the body of Christ is showing forth Who He is.

Let me give you Colossians 2:9 in The Message translation:, *"Everything of God gets expressed in Him, so you can see and hear Him clearly. You don't need a telescope, a microscope, or a horoscope to realize the fullness of Christ, and the emptiness of the universe without Him. When you come to Him, that fullness comes together for you, too. His power extends over everything."*

Entering into this fullness is not something you figure out or achieve. It's not a matter of being circumcised or keeping a long list of laws. No, you're already in—insiders—not through some secretive initiation rite, but rather through what Christ has already gone through for you, destroying the power of sin. There's no power in sin for us, anymore. There's sin, but there's no power; His power is far greater.

And it says, "He dwells and His fullness is all in all." God wants to fill every part of you. God wants to fill every part of this universe with Himself, with His glory. He is filling every part, saying, "I want to assure you of something: that just as when Jesus walked, He had the fullness in Him, you have the fullness in you." You really, really do.

It's a realization of who we've been created to be. And God says, "This is who you've been created to be—My carriers of My glory and My presence, carriers of the fullness of Who I am."

Now that means whatever situation you find yourself in—the fullness of God ready to take care of it. There was never a time where you heard Jesus saying, "Oh, no! What am I going to do now? Hungry people, no food—what were You thinking, God?" Nope—that never happened. In every situation, He understood that there was an ability within Him to take care of, to overcome, to be greater than any circumstance and any situation.

"Just as the Father sent Me, so I send you."

I'm telling you something—we have the same call on our lives that Jesus had on His, and that is to bring forth and manifest the Father. We have the same ability that Jesus had, the same spirit that raised Him from the dead, dwelling in us.

In Ephesians 1:23 it says, *"Which is his body, the fullness of him that filleth all in all."* The fullness of His body Who fills everything and everywhere with Himself.

"Hmmm—maybe the fullness of God is in me. Maybe God fills everything, everywhere with Himself and He fills me—every part of me—with Him. Every part of me with Him."

It's been far too long that we've heard and heard again the message that says, "We're sinners, saved by grace." It's been far too long that we've heard the message, "We're just human. We're nothing but dust. O, God—it's me; the displeasing one to

You." What we're really saying is, "What You did on the cross isn't nearly as powerful as my thoughts about myself are." But God says, "I want you to change your thoughts to agree with My thoughts."

Let me give you Ephesians 1:23 in The Message: *"The church, you see, is not peripheral to the world; the world is peripheral to the church. The church is Christ's body, in which He speaks and acts, by which He fills everything with His presence. Now, according to this, how is God filling everything with His presence? Through us—the body."*

And then it says that the church is not peripheral to the world. The word "peripheral" can best be understood when talking about vision—it means "outside of the normal vision range." He said, "The church is not outside the world, but the center focus of everything is the church, where God expresses Himself, where God shows His glory, where God shows Himself." The world is inside the vision of the church now for the glory and honor of God.

We think we need to perform as society expects. However, we do not have to compare ourselves with society or its standards. We need to demonstrate to the world that what is inside us, the Spirit and the gifts of the Spirit, cannot be duplicated by the best music, lighting, or anything that technology has to offer.

Ephesians 3:19 affirms, *"And to know the love of Christ, which passeth knowledge, that ye might be filled with all the fullness of God."* Knowing the love of Christ, which far surpasses mere knowledge or understanding; so you may be filled with the fullness of God. Ah! A being, a body—me, flooded with God. Flooded with Him! We become those who can bring forth the very things of God. When Jesus said, "When you've seen Me, you've seen the Father," He understood being a body—being in a body—but being filled and flooded with God Almighty Himself. That's a description of us, that's a description of the body of Christ—being flooded and filled with God.

Ephesians 3:19 in The Message: "Live full lives, full in the fullness of God." Now think for just a moment: What is God filled with—wrath and indignation? Anger and disappointment? Sickness and hurt? No. What is God filled with? Love and joy. Peace. Healing. Absolute exuberance. And confidence! That's the God we're filled with.

And He says, "I want you to know that when I came into your lives, I did a complete job." We have a theory in Christianity—we're a work in progress. But in reality our true work is to renew our mind to God's Word, confirming once and for all in our hearts what has already been done. It's not that God the Father, God the Son, God the Holy Spirit are saying, "We still have a lot of work to do with them." No. When He said, "It is finished," He really meant that it's finished. Now it's us, renewing ourselves to who He has made us to be.

I was thinking about this—I know that little girls are made of sugar and spice and everything nice, and little boys are made of, what? Snips and snails and puppy dog tails. But I'm going to tell you what we're made of. We're made of the very same substance that God Himself is. We're hewn from that same Rock. We've been recreated in Christ Jesus, and everything that's in Him is in us.

COMPLETE IN HIM

"Whom we preach, warning every man, and teaching every man in all wisdom; that we may present every man perfect in Christ Jesus," —Colossians 1:28. When the preaching goes forth—when we receive the Word—we actually see that we are complete in Him.

Some time ago, our good friends from Holy Smoke, another ministry we've been friends with for many years, came in and redecorated our church auditorium. When they did, they did everything that needed to be done, start to finish. It would be so very strange for them to come to us today and say, "Hey—we still have to complete the decorating." It'd be strange, because the job was completed already. On the last day of work, when the paint was dry, the clean up was done, they said, "There it is! It is complete."

I want you to know that when God said, "you are complete"

in Him—He meant it. And if we would receive that we are complete, we'd walk in the fullness that He's called us to. 2 Timothy 3:17: "That the man of God may be perfect, thoroughly furnished unto all good works." We're complete, proficient, well fit; we're equipped for every good work.

If I felt it all depended on me to help people, to heal people, to teach people, I'd be terrified. But I know it is God with me and in me—that He will speak through me words that need to be heard. God empowers us to not be on our own, but partners with Him.

Hebrews 13:21 reveals our partnership with Christ, *"Make you perfect in every good work to do his will, working in you that which is well-pleasing in his sight, through Jesus Christ; to whom be glory for ever and ever. Amen."* God has strengthened us, completed us, perfected us, and He Himself (this is so amazing to me), He Himself makes me—makes you—what we ought to be! He said, "I've begun the good work—I will see it to completion."

And in 1 Peter 5:10, *"But the God of all grace, who hath called us unto his eternal glory by Christ Jesus, after that ye have suffered a while, make you perfect, establish, strengthen, settle you."* After you have suffered a little while, the God of all grace, Who has called you to His eternal glory in Christ Jesus, will make you perfect, what you ought to be: established, strengthened, and settled.

I can depend on my Father God to complete—to make me—

what I ought to be. And my job is to open my eyes to what He's done. That's my job, to see who He has created me to be. But it's God Himself who's doing this work in you. Don't get all uptight, "I'm just not growing fast enough!" Well, then open your eyes and see the growth, and see the perfection that He's called you to.

Matthew 5:48 tells us, *"Be ye therefore perfect, even as your Father which is in heaven is perfect."* Now that's a real easy one, isn't it? Be perfect as He's perfect—it's pretty easy, right? Well, let's look at this:

"You therefore must be perfect." When my friend Jessica's mother walked in to my office today, I looked at her and said, "That must be Jessica's mom." Now, I didn't say, "You MUST be her mom." I said, "That must be her mom." They are so much alike—they are obviously related.

And what He's saying in this scripture is: You must be perfect—because, after all, your heavenly Father is perfect! And He's showing us that our perfection comes from Him. It's not about our actions and doing all things perfectly. But if we realize that our perfection comes from Him, then our works become perfect also—because we've awakened unto righteousness. And we no longer have a problem with sin.

He's completed all His work in us. All of creation was spoken forth, and Jesus came as that Living Word, speaking into our lives and making us the creation He's called us to be.

JOY OVERFLOWING

In John 15:11, a joyful truth is revealed, *"These things have I spoken unto you, that my joy might remain in you, and that your joy might be full."* Isn't it amazing? You'd have thought that Jesus would come to make us sorrowful, that He would come to make us really upset at how we've been—but instead He said, "I came to make your joy absolutely complete and overflowing." God likes us to be happy! So much so that He gave me and you His joy.

Here's John 16:24, *"Hitherto have ye asked nothing in my name: ask, and ye shall receive, that your joy may be full."* Up to this time you have not asked for anything in My Name; but now ask and you will receive, so that your joy may be full. He says, "When your prayers are answered, your joy is full and complete." And that's why He says, "Every promise is yes and amen," and again, "Before you've asked—I've answered." It is His good pleasure to give us the kingdom. "I answer your prayer and it makes your joy full." That's Him.

John 17:13, *"And now come I to thee; and these things I speak in the world, that they might have my joy fulfilled in themselves."* Jesus said this when He was about to be crucified: "I say these things while I am still in the world, so that My joy may be made complete and perfect—where? *In* them. This is a desire of the Father—that His delight becomes your delight, that His joy becomes your joy.

That is His delight. That's what He wants! And He says, "That it would be full, complete, and overflowing."

2 Corinthians 1:22 says, *"Who hath also sealed us, and given the earnest of the Spirit in our hearts."* By His Spirit He has stamped us with His eternal pledge—a sure beginning of what He has destined to complete. He said, "I've given you the Holy Spirit. And I'm telling you that I will come back again for that Spirit that is within you." He's my guarantee that this work is incredible here, and that everything will come to a complete end in which He is absolute Lord over everything and everyone. And He says, "This is my promise to you."

"No man hath seen God at any time. If we love one another, God dwelleth in us, and his love is perfected in us," —1 John 4:12. No one has seen God, ever. But if we love one another, God dwells deeply within us, and His love—His love—becomes complete in us—perfect love! So it's God's love. Love unexpressed really isn't love. But when love is expressed, it comes into being.

And God says, "My love—that's Who I am. But I've expressed My love and it's come into being in My body." And when you express God, you express love. He said, "Then My love is complete in you." That's pretty awesome. He says, "I've made you absolutely complete in Me. I've given you everything, the fullness of Who I am. I have perfected you. I've made you whole."

WHOLE & HOLY

Read Psalm 55:18 with me: *"He hath delivered my soul in peace from the battle that was against me: for there were many with me."* My life is well and whole, secure in the middle of danger even while thousands are lined up against me. Now that sounds like how Jesus is... while His betrayal was in progress, He took bread. *"For the joy that was set before Him, He endured the cross."*

And the Psalmist says, "My life is well and whole, secure in the middle of danger." That can't be, unless it's God's nature in us! I can't be secure in the middle of danger—I'm scared! But in the middle of danger, He said, "My nature will come forth, and you'll be secure." Don't worry. It's going to be okay.

You know, there's that commercial: "Aren't you glad you used Dial; don't you wish everybody did?" The commercial in this particular scripture is, "Aren't you glad you know Him; don't you wish everybody did?" When all kinds of havoc is taking place, we can stay calm just like He is calm.

Psalm 119:80, *"Let my heart be sound in thy statutes; that I be not ashamed."* And let me live whole and holy, soul and body, so I can always walk with my head held high. We've seen a lot of things happen in ministry. We've seen a lot of people not walk the walk. But I'm going to tell you about people that have trouble walking the walk—it's not because they're evil. It's not because they're horrid people. Most of the time they don't know the gospel; they don't know what's been done for them.

And therefore they believe that they're still sinners that they're still struggling, and they bring in rules to try to keep them from struggling. "I'm going to do this and I'm going to do that . . ." And they can never keep up with the rules.

When you understand who God has made you to be, sin really, really, isn't a big issue anymore at all. And this Scripture said that He has made you whole, and holy. You've been made holy.

"Well, I'm holy when I do these things"—No, you're not. You're holy because you were born again unto righteousness—you were born again into this, you were recreated holy. He's made me whole and holy.

Ephesians 1:4 reads, *"According as he hath chosen us in him before the foundation of the world, that we should be holy and without blame before him in love."* Long before He laid down earth's foundations, He had us in mind, had settled on us as the focus of His love, to be made whole and holy by His love. He focused it on us—His love. And He said, "Because I love them so much, they're going to be whole and holy. They're Mine."

Isaiah 26:12, *"Lord, thou wilt ordain peace for us: for thou also hast wrought all our works in us."* God, order a peaceful and whole life for us, because everything we've done, you've done for us.

"But you know, God does teach me through my emptiness and through my trials."

God brings you through them, and God does something that purifies you, and so we'll believe Him further and further. He does not want us to stay in trials; we're to go through trials. And where do we go through trials to? To a peaceful and whole state. He says, "I'll be with you when you go through them."

Prepare yourself for Isaiah 55:12: *"For ye shall go out with joy, and be led forth with peace: the mountains and the hills shall break forth before you into singing, and all the trees of the field shall clap their hands."* So in joy, you'll be led into a whole and complete life. The mountains and the hills will lead the parade, bursting with song. All the trees of the forest will join the procession, exuberant with applause. All of creation . . . all of creation knows that it's Him. The mountains know it. The hills know it. The trees know it. So now, the church needs to know it—that it's Him, and that we have His life.

"But now being made free from sin, and become servants to God, ye have your fruit unto holiness, and the end everlasting life," —Romans 6:22. But now that you've found you don't have to listen to sin tell you what to do, and have discovered the delight of listening to God, what a surprise! —A whole, healed, put-together life right now, with more and more of life on the way!

A good example of what I mean would be like this. Your mom tells you, just wait until your dad comes home, then you're really going to get what is coming to you. So you are afraid—afraid to face your dad, afraid it will be a very painful experience. But with God it is never that way. Even if you have made a mistake, He is not going to harm you. No spankings. No sending you to your room. Just love, a future filled with love and life.

Romans 10:10: *"For with the heart man believeth unto righteousness; and with the mouth confession is made unto salvation."* With your whole being you embrace God setting things right, and then you say it, right out loud: "God has set everything right between Him and me!" Do you believe that? He has. He has set everything right—there's nothing between us! There's nothing that God is disappointed in, there's nothing that God is saying, "Well, we're in fellowship except for that, well . . . you know what I'm talking about . . ."

"I've set everything right between us." All you have to do is turn and enter into that. It becomes a reality.

1 Corinthians 6:20: *"For ye are bought with a price: therefore glorify God in your body, and in your spirit, which are God's."* God owns the whole works. So let people see God in and through your body. Where's God seen? In the movie? In the Bible? No—He's seen in and through us.

I see Him! I see Him. When there's something lovely that

comes out of your mouth—people hear Him. They see Him when they see you.

Ephesians 5:26: *"That he might sanctify and cleanse it with the washing of water by the Word."* Christ's love makes the church whole. His words evoke her beauty. Everything He does and says is designed to bring the best out of her.

"I thought everything God says and does is designed to point out how awful she is . . . Right?"

No, He made the church whole. And everything He does and says—everything—is to bring out the best in us. That's a good Father, who loves us so much, Who has perfected us.

"In the body of his flesh through death, to present you holy and unblameable and unreproveable in his sight," —Colossians 1:22. But now, by giving Himself completely at the Cross, actually dying for you, Christ brought you over to God's side and put your lives together, whole and holy in His presence. I like that. He put my life together—I'm on God's side now.

Hebrews 13:20 goes on to say, *"Now the God of peace, that brought again from the dead our Lord Jesus, that great shepherd of the sheep, through the blood of the everlasting covenant."* May God, who puts all things together, makes all things whole, Who made a lasting mark through the sacrifice of Jesus, the sacrifice of blood that sealed the eternal covenant, Who led Jesus, our Great Shepherd, up and alive from the dead . . . Put all things together, made all things whole, because of the sacrifice of Jesus . . . I'm whole; I'm holy because of Him!

"If so be ye have tasted that the Lord is gracious," —I Peter 2:3. Now, like infants at the breast, drink deep of God's pure kindness. Then you'll grow up mature and whole in God. Drink deep of God's kindness! It's God's goodness that leads men to repentance; it's His kindness. One time I told God, "You're so kind to me all the time." He is so kind, and I drink in His kindness. God likes to reveal Who Jesus is, so that we can see who we are. He likes to show us His nature so that we can see what our nature is.

PARTAKERS OF MY GRACE

I was in the prayer closet the other day and God said, "I want to talk to you about something."

And I said, "Okay, I'm listening."

"Many think that they're sinners saved by grace. But I'm going to tell you what I've made you to be: you're grace, saving sinners."

And I began to see some things very clearly—that we've not received who He has created us to be. That we do not just "have" grace—we're Living Grace.

I want you to listen very carefully to who He's created us to be: *"Even as it is meet for me to think this of you all, because I have you in my heart; inasmuch as both in my bonds, and in the defense and confirmation of the gospel, ye all are partakers of my grace,"* —Philippians 1:7. "You are partakers of my grace." Now this wasn't Jesus writing Philippians, was it? Who wrote Philippians? Paul. And yet, Paul said, "Be a partaker of my grace." As though what is God's became his, and he could then distribute that which is the Father's. As though he was the body with the fullness of God, giving it out. So maybe we're not sinners saved by grace—maybe we are grace, saving the sinners.

That's pretty incredible.

Ephesians 4:13 brings home the unity factor, *"Till we all come in the unity of the faith, and of the knowledge of the Son of God, unto a perfect man, unto the measure of the stature of the fullness of Christ."* Until we're moving rhythmically and easily with each other, efficient and graceful in response to God's Son, fully mature adults, fully developed within and without, fully alive like Christ. Now, if 'f-u-l' is added at the end of a word, like "graceFUL"—what does that mean? You are full of grace. I am filled with His grace to give out.

"And Stephen, full of faith and power, did great wonders and miracles among the people," —Acts 6:8. Now Stephen, who was full of

grace (divine blessing) and power, worked great wonders among the people. We're no longer sinners. We read the scriptures and they told us that He took care of sin, and it is powerless—we're no longer sinners, but we are grace going after the sinners to bring them into grace.

We're not the sick—listen to this statement—we're not the sick trying to be healed; we are healing restoring the sick.

"Well, I understand that we're healed."

No, we are healing. You and I, being recreated in Christ, are now a healing spirit. The words that we speak are to bring forth healing. The hands that we have are to bring forth healing. I'm telling you that we are "healing." We are not the "sick, trying to be healed;" we are "healing, restoring the sick."

We are not the unforgiven trying to get forgiveness; we are "forgiveness for the unforgiven."

FORGIVENESS FOR THE UNFORGIVEN

John 20:23 tells us, *"Whosoever sins ye remit, they are remitted unto them; and whosoever sins ye retain, they are retained."* "If you forgive someone's sins, they're gone for good. If you don't forgive sins, what are you going to do with them?"

When Jesus went forth, He went forth with a different authority than anyone had ever seen before. He looked at a man that was sick and He said, "Your sins be forgiven you." And the man got up and was healed. You'd have thought everyone would've been blown away—"Wow! We just saw a miracle!" Because we know—if people see a miracle, they'll come to Jesus.

No, not necessarily so. They saw a miracle, but . . . A man got up that had been in his bed, had been so crippled that his friends had to lower him down from the roof when Jesus said, "Your sins are forgiven you." And instead of seeing that the man got up and was healed, everyone said, "I don't think He has authority to do that. He has no right to do that!"

But Jesus said, "I want to tell you: what would be easier to say, 'be healed' or be forgiven and released of your sins? But so that you would know that the Son of Man has authority, I said 'be released of your sins.'"

In John 21, when Jesus is walking the earth for 40 days after He had died and resurrected, He gives the disciples an authority, and gives you and I an authority, that man had never had before: you can forgive their sins. He's not talking about when somebody's offended you. When somebody's offended you, you have a job—forgive them! But here He's talking about—you and I have a right to forgive sin.

See, we're not those who are agitated, looking for peace—we are peace looking for the agitated to bring in peace. He didn't say when you enter a home "speak the peace of God." He said, "Speak your peace." And whoever is there will be relieved from all the distresses that sin has brought. That's authority.

He said, "You have the right to forgive sin." But see, we've been caught up in "I just need to get God to forgive me . . ." You are forgiveness. Now you've got to bring that message to other people.

We're not the unlovable, trying to be loved; we are love for the unlovable.

LOVE FOR THE UNLOVABLE

"And hope maketh not ashamed; because the love of God is shed abroad in our hearts by the Holy Ghost which is given unto us," — Romans 5:5. Such hope never disappoints or deludes or shames us, for God's love has been poured out in our hearts through the Holy Spirit Who has been given to us. Where's God's love now? It's in us. And what are we supposed to do with that love? Pour it out. Give it to the unlovable.

We're not waiting for God to overshadow us to meet our needs; we are God's shadow, ready to meet the needs of others.

Acts 5:15 SAYS, *"Insomuch that they brought forth the sick into the streets, and laid them on beds and couches, that at the least the shad-*

ow of Peter passing by might overshadow some of them." They brought forth the sick into the streets, laid them on beds and couches, so that at least the shadow of Peter—not the shadow of God, but the shadow of Peter—passing by might overshadow some of them.

Now that's also pretty incredible. Just as the Father overshadowed Jesus and spoke, "This is My beloved Son, in Whom I am well pleased." In speaking this, the Father confirmed that He would meet all the needs of the Son, and the Son would be able to meet the needs of all that came to Him.

Now His shadow is in me. And I become that shadow to overshadow those who need, and those who have needs to be met—we become that shadow. We are not waiting for the water to be stirred to heal us; we are the waters stirred, ready to heal others.

WE ARE THE MIRACLE

John 7:38, *"He that believeth on me, as the scripture hath said, out of his belly shall flow rivers of living water."* He, who believes in Me, shall be a fount of living water. Inside me is living water. Inside you is bubbling-over living water. Now, why did the water get bubbling over, why did it get stirred? So that healing can happen. Wherever we're at, whoever we come in contact with.

We're not waiting for the wind to refresh us; we are the wind refreshing others.

John 3:8 states, *"The wind bloweth where it listeth, and thou hearest the sound thereof, but canst not tell whence it cometh, and whither it goeth: so is every one that is born of the Spirit."* The wind blows (breathes) where it wills; and though you hear its sound, yet you neither know where it comes from, nor where it is going. So it is with everyone who is born of the Spirit. The wind comes and refreshes. The wind comes and clears. And it says, "So it is with everyone." Not just the wind coming on you; you being the wind—refreshing and clearing.

We're not waiting for God's fire to purify us; we are His fire to purify others.

Hebrews 1:7, *"And of the angels he saith, Who maketh his angels spirits, and his ministers a flame of fire."* God makes His angels winds and His ministering servants flames of fire. He says we're to go and ignite wherever we're at, because He calls us "flames of fire." We're not needing a miracle to change our lives; we are the miracle to change the lives of others.

II Corinthians 12:12, *"Truly the signs of an apostle were wrought among you in all patience, in signs, and wonders, and mighty deeds."* All the signs that mark a true apostle were in evidence while I was with you through both good times and bad: signs of portent, signs of wonder, signs of power.

Don't wait for the revival—you are the revival!

Don't wait for the fire—you are the fire!

Don't wait for the healing—you are the healing!

Don't wait for the water to be stirred—you are stirring the waters!

Don't wait for the miracle—you are the miracle.

The keys have been placed in our hands, and we have to understand who we've been created to be. We're not looking for His glory to come on us—we are His glory manifest to others.

2 Peter 1:3 is more proof, *"According as his divine power hath given unto us all things that pertain unto life and godliness, through the knowledge of him that hath called us to glory and virtue."* His divine power has given us all things pertaining to a life in godliness, through the knowledge of Him Who has called us to His glory and virtue. That means the manifest presence of God. Where is the manifest presence of God—the fullness is where? In me. And so, the glory—I become. And I can bring God's manifest presence wherever I go.

We're not looking for a sign to convince us of God's reality—we are the sign to convince others of God's reality.

"God also bearing them witness, both with signs and wonders, and with divers miracles, and gifts of the Holy Ghost, according to his own

will..." —Hebrews 2:4. God showed His approval by signs and wonders and various miracles and by imparting the gives of the Holy Spirit. So, according to the scriptures that we're reading—we are a sign, we are the reality that goes forth and shows people the reality of God.

We're not the weak looking for strength to be empowered; we are strength looking to empower the weak. He's been made unto me strength—therefore we are strength. Philippians 4:13: "I can do all things through Christ which strengtheneth me." I have strength for all things because Christ empowers me.

We're not the spiritually dead, looking for life—we are life looking to resurrect the dead.

"Then Jesus said unto them, Verily, verily, I say unto you, Except ye eat the flesh of the Son of man, and drink his blood, ye have no life in you. Whoso eateth my flesh, and drinketh my blood, hath eternal life; and I will raise him up at the last day." —John 6:53-54. When we die, we will possess Eternal life? No—I possess it now—I now have His life. His very life, the very Zoe of God—I have in me, now!

We're not the brokenhearted looking for wholeness, but we are wholeness looking to restore the brokenhearted.

"And the peace of God, which passeth all understanding, shall keep your hearts and minds through Christ Jesus." —Philippians 4:7. Before you know it, a sense of God's wholeness, everything coming

together for good, will come and settle you down. It's wonderful what happens when Christ displaces worry at the center of your life. Where is worry—it's been displaced. I have a sense of God's wholeness; I am whole.

We are not those without God's word—we are His word for those who are without.

2 Corinthians 3:2 declares, *"Ye are our epistle written in our hearts, known and read of all men."* 1 Thessalonian's 1:8 continues, *"For from you sounded out the Word of the Lord not only in Macedonia and Achaia, but also in every place your faith to God-ward is spread abroad; so that we need not to speak any thing."* The epistle in our hearts, the word, has gotten around. Your lives are echoing the Master's Word, not only in the provinces but all over the place. The news of your faith in God is out. We don't even have to say anything anymore—you're the message! You are the epistle. You are the Word.

We're not the unhearing trying to listen to the voice—we are the voice for the unhearing ones.

John 1:23 quotes John the Baptist: *"He said, I am the voice of one crying in the wilderness, Make straight the way of the Lord, as said the prophet Isaiah."* John didn't have a voice—he was the voice. You don't just have a voice—you are the voice.

We are not the unredeemed without the living blood—we are

the living blood for the unredeemed.

"The cup of blessing which we bless, is it not the communion of the blood of Christ? The bread which we break, is it not the communion of the body of Christ?" —I Corinthians 10:16. When we drink the cup of blessing, aren't we taking into ourselves the blood, the very life, of Christ? And isn't it the same with the loaf of bread we break and eat? Don't we take into ourselves the body of Christ?

The blood speaks—not from the ground; the blood speaks from this earth. It speaks from our mouth. We are the blood speaking.

"From whom the whole body fitly joined together and compacted by that which every joint supplieth, according to the effectual working in the measure of every part, maketh increase of the body unto the edifying of itself in love," —Ephesians 4:16. He keeps us in step with each other. His very Breath and Blood flow through us, nourishing us so that we will grow up healthy in God, robust in love.

His very Blood flows through us.

We're not darkness, looking for light—we are the light entering into those dark areas.

We're not the unredeemed—we're the redeemed!

We're not the sinners—we're the righteous!

We're not the sick—we're the healed!

It's called the gospel! ❈

www.ingramcontent.com/pod-product-compliance
Lightning Source LLC
LaVergne TN
LVHW051500080426
835509LV00017B/1845